WEATHER Secrets and Signs

Simon Keeling

WEATHER
Secrets and Signs

An everyday guide to understanding and predicting our weather

National Trust

Published by National Trust Books
An imprint of HarperCollins Publishers,
1 London Bridge Street London SE1 9GF
www.harpercollins.co.uk

HarperCollins Publishers,
Macken House,
39/40 Mayor Street Upper,
Dublin 1, D01 C9W8, Ireland

First published 2026

ISBN 978-0-00-880418-3
10 9 8 7 6 5 4 3 2 1

A catalogue record for this book is available from the British Library.

Printed and bound in India by Replika Press Pvt. Ltd.
If you would like to comment on any aspect of this book, please contact us at the above address or national.trust@harpercollins.co.uk

National Trust publications are available at National Trust shops or online at nationaltrustbooks.co.uk

MIX
Paper | Supporting responsible forestry
FSC™ C016779
FSC www.fsc.org

Contents

Introduction

Having a day out in the British Isles? The weather forecast will invariably be one of the first items on your list as you plan whether it's T-shirt and shorts, jumper and trousers, sandals or walking boots.

The weather impacts us every day, both indoors and outside. Ever-changing from day to day, month to month, season to season, the weather provides a constant yet shifting backdrop to everything we do. It charts the timeline of our lives and colours our experiences and memories.

In this book I want to show you how, following some easy rules, you can create your own weather forecasts. Apps on our mobile phones are useful, but there is no way an app can make an accurate prediction for your specific location. You, however, can! Knowledge of the broader weather picture can enable you to use your own experience to decide whether rain is a few minutes or hours away, whether it will snow or the sun will come out. By noticing and observing changes in the weather, equipped with the tools and techniques to understand what those changes mean, we can strengthen our ties to the natural world and begin to appreciate the impact that weather has on it.

Weather is a description of the conditions we are experiencing now and in the near future. It encompasses the sun, rain, sleet and snow that we may encounter on any given day; temperatures of a cold winter and a warm summer. It differs from climate, which is the term we use to describe a long-term average of weather conditions over years, decades, centuries and millennia.

Since time began the climate of the Earth has changed. Evidence of ice ages and long-past hotter conditions are all around us. Epochs of weather are well known, allowing the flora and fauna of those times to flourish, before new plants and creatures evolved to thrive in a climate as it is now. Human activity is accelerating climate change, and life on Earth is being challenged more than ever before. You can find out more about our changing climate, and the National Trust's work, on page 136.

Despite a changing climate, our ability to observe nature, read the signs and make forecasts remains firmly intact. With a little knowledge and a bit of practice, you will soon know what to look out for and how to make accurate predictions.

Over the following pages you will learn how to identify clouds and interpret what they mean; understand how rainbows are formed; measure wind speeds without any equipment; discover what brings rain or snow; forecast a thunderstorm; learn how to sense fog before it arrives; read the lines and symbols on weather maps; and find out which official forecasts you can trust. There's also a chance to test out those old sayings we're all familiar with (red sky at night ... too cold to snow ... lightning never strikes twice) and find out if they are true or false.

The weather may be a force to be reckoned with but, by tuning into its changes and learning to interpret its secrets and signs, we can anticipate and adapt to its shifting moods with greater confidence, armed with the answer to that endlessly intriguing question: what will happen next?

CHAPTER 1

THE BIG PICTURE

When it's raining outside we can easily imagine it's wet everywhere – but of course it isn't. Taking a step back and viewing the atmosphere as a whole is key to understanding the weather. Looking at images of Earth from space reveals seemingly chaotic spirals of cloud, but watch a sequence of these pictures and you will soon see how each spiral interacts with the next.

This interaction is the 'weather machine' at work, and the exchange of particles of air between these spirals is what shapes our weather.

How the atmosphere works

A spinning blue ball in the vastness of space. That's us. Earth.

Surrounded by blackness, and as far as we are aware, alone, Earth has been spinning in space for around 4 billion years. Conforming to the known laws of physics, the planet has an atmosphere that clings to it courtesy of gravity.

Other planets have atmospheres too, although (at least for now) none that we know of has an atmosphere like ours, capable of supporting life.

Earth's atmosphere is made up of several gases: mostly nitrogen (78 per cent), oxygen (21 per cent) and smaller amounts of other gases. The most important of these other gases, when thinking about weather, is water vapour (the amount of it varies on a daily basis).

This mixture of gases wraps around Earth as it spins. Although there's no abrupt line where the atmosphere of Earth ends and space begins, most of the atmosphere in which we exist is in an incredibly thin layer called the **troposphere**. Just 7 miles deep, it provides all that's needed for life, and for weather to exist.

← Earth is the only known planet with an atmosphere capable of supporting life.

↗ A view of the stratosphere.

More on the atmosphere

The troposphere is just one layer of the atmosphere, but the most important for life on Earth. It's where we live and where most weather occurs. Temperatures fall with height in the troposphere, as you may have noticed if you have travelled on a jet aircraft and witnessed ice forming on windows as you climb.

An abrupt boundary known as the tropopause marks the start of the next layer, the **stratosphere**, which extends to about 30 miles above the surface. This is a dry layer where, instead of continuing to fall, temperature increases with height. It's within the stratosphere that we find the ozone layer, which absorbs a significant portion of the sun's harmful ultraviolet radiation, ultimately making life on Earth possible.

Next comes the **mesosphere**, where temperatures fall again, as low as around -160°C, and extending to 60 miles above the ground. It's in the mesosphere that shooting stars burn up. It's a difficult atmospheric layer to study because it's too high for research aircraft and balloons but too low for orbiting satellites. However, we know it has a sizeable impact on the weather we experience as atmospheric gravity waves pass through, expanding and contracting the air.

Above these levels are the **thermosphere** and the **exosphere**, each performing a function as part of the complex structure of the Earth's atmosphere before slowly merging with space.

Global circulation

Hadley, Ferrel and Polar Cells

The Earth's axis is offset by about 23 degrees, which leads to the sun unevenly heating the surface. As it spins, the Earth 'wobbles' and the spinning results in an easterly movement of air known as the **Coriolis effect**, one of many forces in play. Oceans and land masses further enhance the seeming randomness of the atmosphere.

We can make some sense of this apparent chaos. The factors above (and others) combine to create circulation cells, which are mirrored in the northern and southern hemispheres.

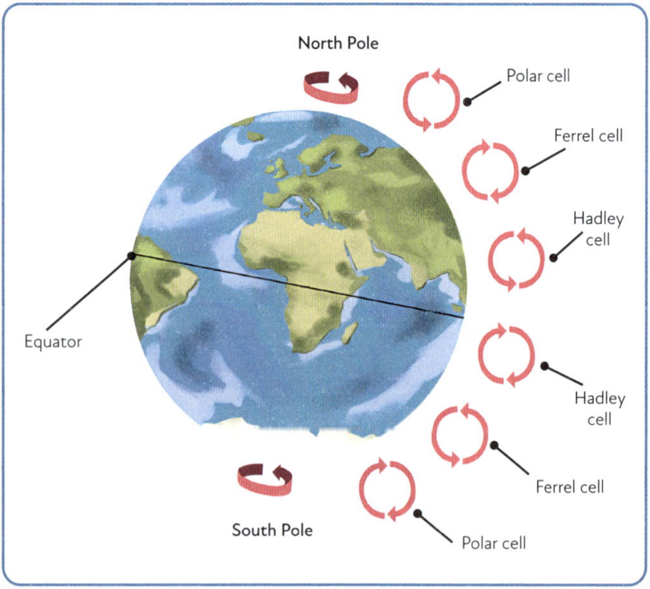

These cells are formed by air being heated and rising, then cooling and sinking. Where the air rises we find areas of **low pressure** aligned in regions around the globe. Where the air sinks is where we find **high pressure** regions. Two of the cells of rising and sinking air are named after the scientists that suggested their existence: the Hadley cell and the Ferrel cell. The other is known as the Polar cell. Each of the cells are replicated in the northern and southern hemispheres.

Working our way from the equator, the **Hadley cell** is the largest and extends (in the northern hemisphere) north from the equator to above the latitude of Spain and Portugal. As air rises over the Intertropical Convergence Zone (where the trade winds of the northern and southern hemispheres meet) it forms huge thunderstorms. Air from the top of these storms flows north, cools and then sinks, producing high pressure in the subtropics, such as over the Azores in the Atlantic Ocean.

As we head north we then meet the smaller **Ferrel cell**. Now, imagine the air in these cells constantly circulating; there is no stop or start. Warm air from the subtropical high (an area of high atmospheric pressure) flows north towards the mid-Atlantic and it meets cooler air moving south from the North Pole. Where these two surface winds meet the air is forced to rise again, usually around the same latitude as the British Isles. The rising air cools, forming areas of low pressure bringing clouds and rain. It's also responsible for the **jet stream** and the weather **fronts** (think of 'fronts' as areas of cloud and rain – see Chapter 8) that we see affecting these latitudes. At high levels the air returns south, eventually sinking back into the Hadley cell and making the subtropical high even stronger.

And then there is the **Polar cell**. This is the weakest and smallest of the atmospheric circulation cells. Cold, dense air at the North and South Poles creates high pressure here. Air flows from the high pressure area over the poles (this high pressure is why the polar regions are dry), flowing south at the surface to meet the Ferrel cell winds. Where these two meet is where we find the unsettled area of low pressure, wind and rain, as well as the jet stream that we call the Polar Front jet stream.

Jet streams

Think of the jet stream as a strong, but not consistent, tube of wind that meanders around the globe at high levels, about 5–7 miles above the surface of the Earth.

The main jet streams are the **Polar jet stream** (which affects the North Atlantic and therefore the British Isles), the **Subtropical jet stream** and the **Tropical jet stream**, the latter being the only one blowing from east to west, the other two blowing west to east. There are local jet streams that can occur in much smaller geographical areas, but we won't go into these here.

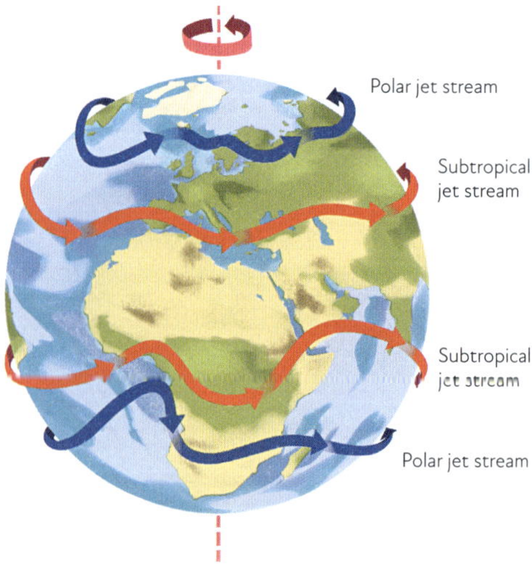

The main function of a jet stream is to aid the exchange of cold, dry air from the poles with moist, warm air from the equator. The temperature difference where the two air blocks meet causes the wind to blow strongly in the jet stream, over 200mph during winter.

The Polar jet stream enhances low pressure and fronts; it's responsible for our changeable weather in the British Isles and all areas on the boundary of the Ferrel and Polar cells.

Subtropical jet streams help the development of storm systems, including monsoons, which bring welcome rainfall to tropical areas, as well as influencing the weather systems in the Ferrel cell regions.

Finally, the easterly flowing Tropical jet stream occurs from around late June to early September. It flows from South East Asia to Africa and helps form hurricanes, moving them off the coasts of West Africa and into the Atlantic.

It's all linked

No one part of global circulation acts in isolation. Each of the features of Earth's circulation interacts and has an impact on other features. This is one of the reasons for the complexity of forecasting, whether predicting the weather of the next few hours or the climate of decades to come.

FACTS ABOUT GLOBAL CIRCULATION

1. At the equator the Earth spins at about 1,000mph; it spins near 0mph at the poles.

2. On the same day the temperature at the poles can be close to -60°C, while areas close to the equator are over 40°C.

3. The fastest recorded wind speed in a jet stream was 258mph, near Yonago, Japan on 5 February 2004.

CHAPTER 2

CLOUDS

They are in the sky almost every day. Look up and these white masses are floating around, telling us what the weather will bring.

While each individual cloud shape is unique, when categorised into simple groups they can help us make sense of the weather they predict.

Clouds are nature's most reliable tools for forecasting, whether they're fluffy or flat, completely covering the sky or thin white wisps high up in the atmosphere. Learning a few shapes and seeing how they change will reward the watcher with a lifetime of forecasting know-how – and the perfect excuse to sit and stare.

On a December evening in London in 1802, a quiet, young amateur meteorologist by the name of Luke Howard presented a lecture entitled 'On the Modifications of Clouds'. Following this lecture, Howard's life and that of meteorological science were about to change for ever.

Howard was not the first person to attempt the seemingly unachievable goal of cataloguing what could well have been a random series of cloud forms; this had been done before. But Howard was the first to make the grouping of clouds logical, simple and relatively easy to use.

Think of the sky being the canvas on which the weather paints. Ever-changing cloud bases, depth, shape and appearance tell us all we need to know about the state of the atmosphere at any particular moment, and what might be the weather of the coming hours and, sometimes, days.

↑ A thunderstorm approaching.

Cloud watching is perhaps the perfect excuse to sit, staring up at the sky, observing the evolution of cloud structures as the atmosphere slowly reveals its secrets. Even a few seconds of looking broadly at the sky can tell us much about what could happen next.

How many times have you seen a cloud quickly turn darker and the wind increase, bringing a cool rush of air? Next thing you know a shower has arrived and now it's thundering. Notice the bottom of the cloud; see it has a greenish hue? That's a sure sign that hail is imminent. And then, almost as quickly as it came, the precipitation stops, the sky brightens and the temperature increases again.

Each of the steps above denotes a process under way in the atmosphere, all of which can be spotted quickly and easily. More importantly, every stage tells us about what might happen next.

What is a cloud?

First, though, let us consider what we are actually looking at when we observe clouds.

We are surrounded by an atmospheric 'ocean' which consists of various gases. Some of these gases keep us alive and some determine the weather.

The most important of the gases when thinking about clouds is water vapour. This invisible gas is around us all of the time. It's only when the temperature drops low enough that water vapour changes from an invisible gas into a visible liquid.

This process is called condensation and we see the results of

↓ Condensing water is seen as mist and fog.

it, if it occurs at the Earth's surface, as mist and fog. More usually condensation occurs above the surface and we then see the water droplets as clouds.

The atmosphere can only hold so much water as an invisible vapour for any given temperature. Therefore if we keep the amount of water vapour the same, then lower the temperature sufficiently, eventually the vapour will condense and we will see this as mist or cloud.

Should the temperature be increased again, reaching the point at which the atmosphere can hold water as an invisible vapour, evaporation takes place and our water droplet 'disappears', becoming a gas again.

This change in temperature is critical to the appearance and disappearance of clouds.

How clouds form

For clouds to form we usually look for areas where air rises or there's a change in temperature. There are two main processes that allow cloud to develop: **convection** and **dynamic lifting**. Whilst this may sound complex, the process is actually rather simple.

First, think of convection as like the steam that comes out of a boiling kettle. Switch on the kettle and the water is heated (the same effect as the sun shining on the surface of the Earth on a summer's day).

Now, focussing on the atmosphere, if the sun heats the ground it will eventually release a bubble of warm air. Since warm air is less dense than cold air, and our bubble is now warmer than the air that surrounds it, the bubble will begin to rise. As we gain height, the temperature of the atmosphere falls. Our bubble also cools as it rises, but, as long as it stays warmer than its surrounding air, it will continue to rise in the atmosphere.

← Convection from a steam train causing 'clouds' to form as warm, moist air leaves the engine and condenses when it meets the cooler air outside.

↑ Air being forced to rise over the hills of north-west Wales forms a line of cumulus clouds.

Eventually the bubble reaches a temperature at which water within the atmosphere can no longer be invisible. Condensation takes place and, as described above, we see that process as cloud. In this case the clouds will be white, fluffy cumulus clouds, which are synonymous with convection (see much more about cumulus clouds on page 32). Collectively, clouds formed by convection are known as 'cumuliform' clouds.

The second type of cloud formation occurs when air gets 'dynamically lifted'. As already described, warm air is less dense than cold air. Should warm, less dense air come up against cold, more dense air, the warmer, lighter air has a tendency to be forced above the colder, denser air. This 'forcing' upwards of the less dense air usually means it's pushed into colder parts of the atmosphere and so again condensation takes place. The water vapour condenses and becomes a liquid droplet that's visible as cloud.

This time the cloud is usually not fluffy but is rather flat. These are the cirrus and stratus clouds (see pages 27 and 35) usually associated with fronts. They're often characterised by being rather featureless, although they will produce the continuous rain usually associated with well-developed low pressure systems.

How to watch clouds

Grab a comfy chair, pour yourself a glass of something pleasant and look up: the best way to learn about clouds is by watching them. Even within a few seconds one can notice subtle changes in clouds, especially where parts of the cloud are forming or disappearing. Usually it's at the extremities of the cloud (the bottom and the top) that we see most changes.

As you watch, notice how the clouds are moving. They are being blown by the wind. At lower levels, clouds in the British Isles will usually be travelling at around 20–30mph. At higher levels, wispy cirrus clouds can be whizzing along at 200mph.

Take notice of how the amount of cloud changes too. Meteorologists estimate cloud cover in eighths. We imagine the sky as a disc, segmented into eight 'wedges'. We then imagine pushing all of the cloud into one section of the sky disc and estimate how many of the equal wedges we have filled.

So, an overcast sky is said to have eight-eighths cloud cover, half of the sky covered in cloud is equivalent to four-eighths cloud cover and a sky completely free of cloud has zero-eighths cloud cover.

Look at how the cloud forms are changing. Are the clouds fluffy, flat, or perhaps a mix of both? Use your phone to take pictures to refer back to later, or scribble in a notebook about the cloud and what you think it might indicate, as well as how much of it there is.

↗ Overcast sky.

↗ Four-eighths of cloud cover; half the sky covered.

→ A rare clear-sky day.

Types of clouds and what they mean

The genius of Luke Howard was to classify clouds by putting them into three height groups: high, medium and low. He then decided on ten main cloud types.

It takes some practice to estimate the height of clouds, but identifying them is much easier. Here are the types you need to know.

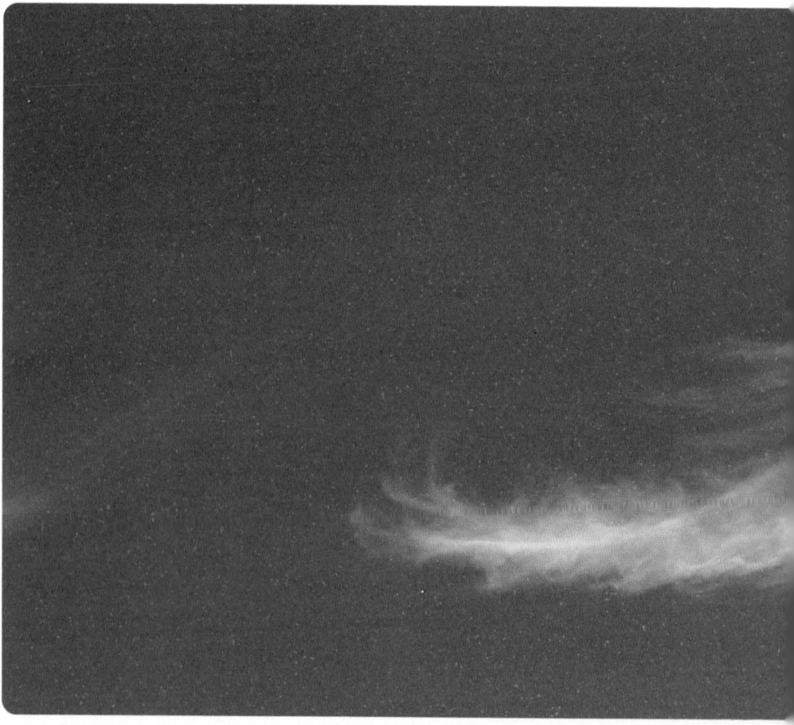

High clouds (above 16,500 feet)

↓ Cirrus

High, wispy clouds, cirrus are the familiar 'hook' type clouds that we see on a summer's day. They occur at around 20,000 feet and, amazingly, are made up of what's known as super-cooled water. This water exists as a liquid, even though temperatures are as low as -40°C.

Watch cirrus clouds carefully. If they're fairly stable as you watch them there's unlikely to be much of a change in the weather. If they're increasing and becoming less 'hooky', it's a sure sign that the weather is deteriorating and rain may be on the way.

↑ Cirrostratus

When cirrus clouds have lost their 'hooks' they frequently evolve into cirrostratus clouds. Occurring at levels of around 15,000–20,000 feet, such clouds appear rather flat and milky, the sun slowly disappearing behind them. Sometimes a halo can form around the sun or moon as they shine through the clouds, caused by light being bent by the water within the cloud. If evolving from cirrus cloud, cirrostratus continue to highlight that a front is on the way and that rain could occur within the next 4–6 hours.

→ Cirrocumulus

These high-level 'lumpy' clouds indicate that the atmosphere is in a showery mood. They often indicate that thunderstorms may occur. There won't be lots of this cloud type, rather patches of them, but it's the storms and showers they foretell that is important.

Medium clouds

(6,500–16,500 feet)

→ Altocumulus

We are now into what we call medium-level clouds and the first of these is altocumulus.

Appearing as small 'lumpy' clouds, often grouped into 'plates', most altocumulus occur between 6,500–16,500 feet. They are part of the cloud sequence of an approaching **warm front** and can be spectacularly beautiful if the sun or moon is visible through them.

Sometimes the altocumulus can have more depth to them and when this happens they look like the turrets of a castle. This cloud is known as altocumulus castellanus and can hint that showers and thunderstorms may break out.

→ Altostratus

Still in the medium levels, altostratus clouds are flatter in appearance than altocumulus. They are usually quite uniform and they tend to occur after altocumulus when ahead of a warm front.

They are opaque clouds, and the sun or moon will often disappear behind them.

If associated with a front, altostratus clouds will often give its first rain. This is usually only light rain but will become more persistent as the front gets closer.

Low clouds (surface– 6,500 feet)

↓ Cumulus

Low clouds are defined as all clouds occurring below 6,500 feet. The archetypal cotton-wool cloud, cumulus can look as if they are not real but have been placed in the sky to make a perfect picture.

Formed by convection (as described on page 22), these clouds depend on the surrounding air being colder than the bubble of air that forms the cloud. The cooler the surrounding air is, and the more moist, the bigger the cumulus can grow. If it grows sufficiently deep, showers may begin to fall. The deeper the cloud, the heavier the showers will be.

↑ Cumulonimbus

These are probably the most famous of clouds. Extending high into the atmosphere, cumulonimbus can extend to more than 40,000 feet in depth.

They are the only clouds that produce thunderstorms and hail, and are also often associated with strong gusts of wind.

Famous for their anvil-shaped tops, cumulonimbus can grow into the levels that passenger aircraft fly at, so frequently a flight path will be changed in order to fly around these cloud tops.

Cumulonimbus clouds tell us the atmosphere is in a very angry state. The weather can change quickly, with the air rising and falling rapidly.

↑ Nimbostratus

Literally meaning 'rain bearing', nimbostratus is associated with warm fronts and persistent rain. With ragged bases, these clouds shroud hills and coasts and bring grey, wet days.

The cloud bottom can be just above the surface of the ground, but may extend 15,000 feet into the atmosphere. This depth of cloud allows for the rain to be moderate or even heavy at times, although it may not last long as it tends to be concentrated along the line of the front itself.

Despite bringing such unsettled weather, nimbostratus tell of better weather ahead; once it has passed, the more persistent rain will fade and give way to cloud and drizzle.

➜ Stratocumulus

With a grey appearance, stratocumulus clouds indicate that the weather is unlikely to be changing much in the coming hours. Referred to as 'pancake' in appearance, these clouds typically have small breaks in them through which the sun may show.

Winds are often light under stratocumulus clouds, although if the wind picks up the cloud will break and this should alert us to a change of weather; this could be more sunshine or perhaps an approaching front.

← Stratus

The lowest of all clouds, stratus can be thought of as fog that has been lifted slightly above the ground. It's a grey, uniform, almost featureless, cloud. There can be times during the winter months when stratus clouds can last for many days, especially if there's a light wind to keep the fog from settling at surface levels.

Usually not very deep, stratus cloud can produce drizzle. If it appears to be raining from stratus, this tells us that there's another cloud, above the stratus, causing the rain.

Stratus cloud also occurs behind a warm front, in the section of the frontal sequence we call the 'warm sector'. Here the cloud can break, more often in the summer months, and if it does then the sun gets through and it can become very warm.

Unusual clouds

↓ Noctilucent

These are thin clouds that occur high in the mesosphere, about 200,000 feet above the surface, and are seen around sunset and twilight.

They often look like cirrus clouds, and in the northern hemisphere they're most often seen between May and August. They can only be seen between latitudes of 45°–80° N. For the clouds to form, a temperature of lower than -120°C is needed and this is why they only occur in summer when temperatures in the mesosphere are at their lowest.

The reason why they form is fascinating: at such a high level, the dust particles they form on may well, in part, be due to meteors being destroyed as they enter Earth's atmosphere, and the water vapour coming from 'gaps' in the troposphere.

Once you see these clouds you can't forget them; they are beautiful.

↑ Mother-of-pearl

Rare in the British Isles, mother-of-pearl clouds (officially called nacreous clouds) occur high in the stratosphere and need temperatures of below -78°C to form.

They appear as iridescent cloud of many colours and are best seen at sunrise and sunset, with the tiny ice crystals within them diffracting sunlight and allowing the beautiful colours to show.

← Rainbow

Not a cloud, but the most recognisable of sky phenomena. Rainbows have been studied since ancient times; in AD 65, the Roman philosopher Seneca correctly noted that they always appear opposite the sun.

Most rainbows occur when the sun hits water droplets at an angle of 42 degrees in front of our eyes. The rainbow will usually happen when the sun is behind us, but a bright moon can cause a rainbow too.

As the sunlight (or moonlight) enters a water droplet it's reflected into the back of the droplet. As it leaves the droplet the light is refracted again and splits out into its constituent parts, and we see this as a rainbow.

The rainbow is actually a full circle; if you look at a rainbow from an aircraft you can sometimes see this.

It's amazing to think that the colours we see are only one part of the rainbow – visible light. There are other forms of 'light' within the rainbow which we cannot see including ultraviolet, gamma radiation and radio waves. Imagine being able to see a rainbow across all of those wavelengths.

FACTS ABOUT CLOUDS

1 Clouds move at an average speed of around 30mph.

2 The lifespan of a cumulus cloud is around 20 minutes, although they often morph into other clouds or rejuvenate into new cumulus clouds.

↑ Fogbow

A beautiful effect created by mist and fog, this is caused by light being bent in very small water droplets that are causing the mist or fog, rather than larger raindrops that cause a rainbow to form.

It looks like a low, broad rainbow but is only white in colour (although sometimes a very thin red band of light can be seen on the outside of the fogbow).

To see the fogbow, the observer needs to have the sun (or moon) behind them and the water droplets in front.

By observing and noting cloud types you will soon become confident in forecasting the weather.

3 Clouds are heavy; an average cumulus weighs 500 tonnes.

4 Seeing shapes or objects in clouds is known as 'pareidolia'.

5 Clouds on other planets are mostly made of sulphur dioxide, cosmic dust, helium, hydrogen and plasma.

WEATHER LORE – TRUE OR FALSE?

For our ancestors the sky provided an ever-changing window into the intentions of the weather and what phenomena may be ahead in the coming hours. A watchful eye on the sky could decide that today is the day for sowing, or mean the difference between harvesting in dry or wet weather.

'Mackerel sky and mare's tails make tall ships carry low sails'

This popular nautical proverb dates back to when different cloud types were used to determine how a ship should trim its sails. 'Mackerel sky' – so named because of its resemblance to fish scales – is associated with altocumulus clouds, which often signify warm, moist air in the middle atmosphere that's in turn associated with thunderstorms. 'Mare's tails' are a type of cirrus cloud, which are also associated with changing weather conditions. Both types can be a sign that windy or stormy weather is approaching, leading any sensible ship's captain to haul in the sails.

'If clouds move against the wind, rain will follow'

Clouds do not really move 'against' the direction of the wind. Winds at higher altitudes may sometimes move in a different direction from that on the ground (this is called 'wind shear') and so higher-altitude clouds will move in this direction rather than follow the directions of the wind in the lower atmosphere. This indicates an unstable atmosphere that can herald the arrival of a cold front, and usually rain.

'The higher the clouds, the fairer the weather'

Generally speaking, higher clouds, such as wispy cirrus, are indicative of good weather – especially if they're changing very little. Even if they do change and rain is on its way, there will usually be a few hours of dry weather ahead.

'When clouds appear like rocks and towers, the Earth's refreshed with frequent showers'

Large, white clouds, reminiscent of towers of stones, castle turrets or cauliflower heads, can contain a lot of dynamic weather. If the clouds start to grow larger and heavier at the base, and take on a greyish tint, then a rain shower or a thunderstorm is likely to be on its way.

'In the morning mountains, in the afternoon fountains'

On a day when there are likely to be showers it doesn't take much heating from the sun for cumulus clouds to build. If these are seen to be growing from early morning, it can be a sign that they will grow into large cumulonimbus clouds ('mountains') bringing heavy showers, gusty winds, hail and thunderstorms.

CHAPTER 3

WINDS

The relief of a cooling sea breeze on a hot summer's day is one of nature's gifts. Then again, a cold breeze on an already freezing day feels like nature has other plans for us!

Strong winds may break up a cloud layer, while light winds might allow mist or fog to form.

By observing the wind, estimating its speed and assessing its direction we can predict how warm (or cold) the weather will be, and whether the day ahead will be wet or dry.

Where the wind blows

↑ Even smoke from a chimney will show the direction of the wind.

Aristotle believed that the winds were caused by 'exhalations' from the Earth and that a hot wind was caused by the sun's heat vaporising water, while cold winds were associated with damp conditions and moist vapour.

It's interesting when reading what Aristotle thought to see that at least he had tried to inject some scientific reasoning into his beliefs. However, he was wrong in his assumptions.

The wind is caused by temperature differences across the Earth; these create changes in pressure that we feel as the wind.

There are two aspects of the wind that have most impact on our day-to-day lives: direction and speed. The forecasting of these two parameters has been vital to human economic activity, from shipping and agriculture to aviation and energy efficiency.

The direction from which the wind blows presents vital clues as to atmospheric conditions in the hours and days ahead, whilst estimating wind speeds predicts how quickly rain or showers may pass through our area.

The wind blows constantly and takes on the characteristics of the surface (sea or land) over which it passes. Knowing a wind's origins helps us tell the story of the air over us at any given time.

Complicated equipment isn't needed to see from where the wind is blowing; even smoke will do. And for wind speed we have the ever-useful Beaufort Wind Scale (see page 53).

Hot or cold, wet or dry?

In the northern hemisphere a wind that's coming from a northerly quadrant is generally expected to be cold. A wind coming from the southern side of the compass is expected to be warm. This is what we would anticipate, given the location of the North Pole and the equator.

As the name tells us, the British Isles are islands; we are surrounded by the sea and so the air always has moisture available to it, though some wind directions are more moist than others.

A wind blowing from the west is coming off the Atlantic and is exposed to vast amounts of water vapour that can turn to cloud and rain.

Winds blowing from the east or south are likely to be drier, having travelled over far less ocean. A wind coming from warmer climes can hold more water and so may be cloudier, unless it has travelled over land before reaching us.

➜ Warm dry winds passing over the desert reach the British Isles from the south.

Sea breezes

On a warm summer's day at the beach, the sea breeze can bring that cooling relief we may desperately need. It's one of the most recognisable features of weather near the coast. Caused by the temperature difference between the land and the sea, this breeze occurs during the months when that contrast is greatest, i.e. between April and August in the British Isles.

We have all experienced how temperatures rise over land during the day, often from a chilly morning to a hot afternoon. Over the sea, and some large lakes, that change in temperature is much less pronounced. It isn't unusual to find temperatures varying by 20°C in a day over land, but by less than 1°C in a day over the sea.

As the air over the land heats up it becomes less dense, rises upwards and drops in pressure. This creates a 'hole' in the atmosphere over the land. The air over the sea is more dense than

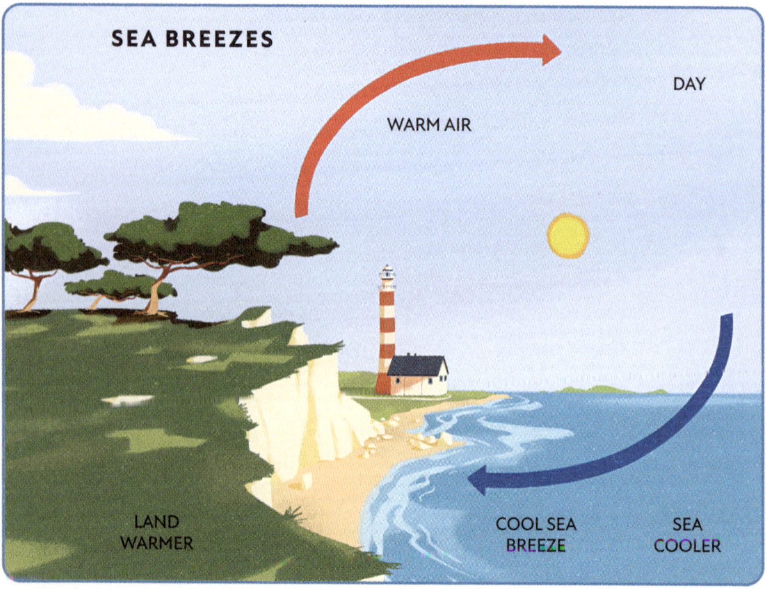

inland and therefore pressure is higher. As air flows from high to low pressure, the wind starts to flow from off the sea towards the land. A circulation is then established.

Sometimes the sea breeze can be strong, arriving with gusty winds. It certainly brings cooler weather, and can sometimes even cause showers to form as clouds develop along the coast.

The sea breeze will penetrate inland around the British Isles and can sometimes make it as far as 90 miles before fading away as temperatures over land decrease again in the evening, and the balance between land and sea temperatures is restored.

Land breezes

The opposite of the sea breeze, the land breeze occurs at night when the land cools down and the sea remains warm.

The cool air that develops over land, as heat escapes into the

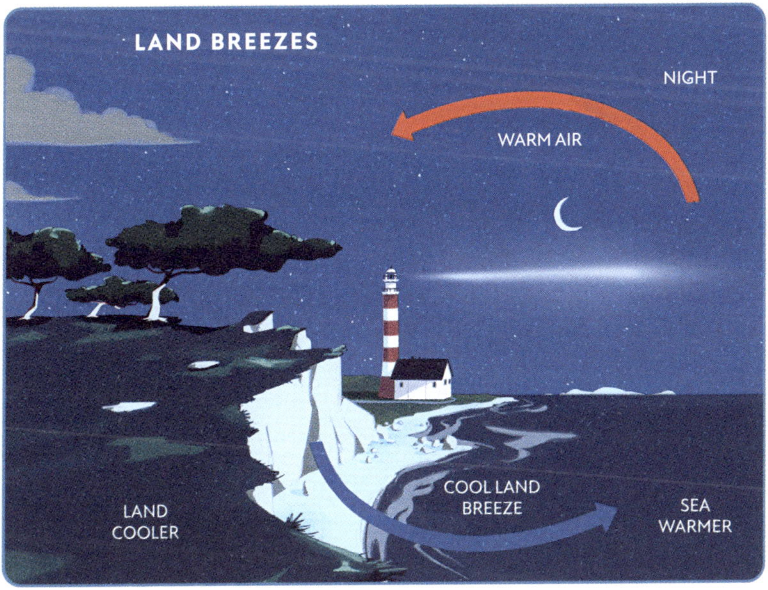

atmosphere, becomes less dense than the warm air over the sea. This causes pressure over the land to rise and become higher than over the sea. As air once again flows from high to low pressure, a land breeze develops, flowing from the land to the sea.

Land breezes, like sea breezes, tend to form during spring and autumn, when temperature contrasts are greatest. However, they can occur at any time of year as long as the sea temperature and land temperature are sufficiently different.

River valleys are favoured exit routes for land breezes, enabling the dense, colder land air to flow out to the warmer sea.

Foehn winds

Foehn winds are warm, dry breezes that occur to the side of hills and mountains protected from the wind, and can happen at any time of the year.

As air flows over high ground, it's forced to rise upwards. As it rises the moisture within the air is squeezed out, forming cloud and possibly causing rain to fall.

By the time it passes the top of the mountain, the air is dry. It then 'falls' down the opposite side, but, because all the moisture has been taken from it, the sky often clears and the sun comes out.

As the air sinks it becomes warmer and so we can have days, especially in the summer months, when places sheltered from a moist airflow can often have fine, warm, sunny days, whilst on the opposite side of the hill or mountain it's cloudy, wet and cool.

A very good example in the British Isles is east of the Highlands and Grampians in Scotland. Similar effects can be seen almost anywhere that a location is sheltered from the wind by high ground.

FOEHN
WINDS
COOL
MOIST AIR
WARM
DRY AIR

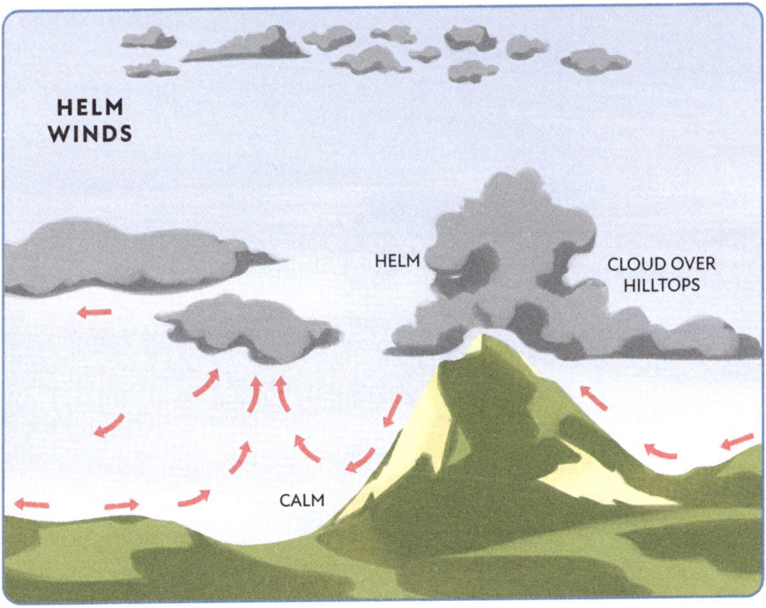
HELM
WINDS
HELM
CLOUD OVER
HILLTOPS
CALM

Helm winds

A roaring wind can be heard on some days in Penrith, Cumbria in England. If the wind is coming from an easterly direction, this is likely to be the helm wind, which is actually a type of foehn wind.

The only wind with a specific name that occurs in the British Isles, the helm wind is well known across northern England. Air from the North Sea is forced to rise over Cross Fell in the northern Pennines. This causes the air to cool and cloud to form over the hilltops, before racing down the westward slopes into the Eden Valley.

Most common in late winter and spring, the helm can be strong enough to knock over walkers and livestock. Many tales are told of this wind, and the use of the name 'helm' is used to describe similarly formed winds across the Lake District and Pennines.

Trade winds

Well known to sailors, the trade winds are part of the global air circulation. They occur north and south of the equator, and through the year they move north and south with the sun as it gets higher and lower in the sky.

The trade winds were named by sailors for the assistance they gave when navigating, assisting with global trade from the eighteenth century.

Occurring throughout the year, 'the trades' are now mainly used by leisure sailors, who rely on them as they cross the Atlantic from Europe to the Caribbean.

← Traditional sailing ships used the trade winds.

🠝 The calm winds of the doldrums could leave sailing ships stranded for weeks.

The doldrums

In the area where the trade winds from the northern hemisphere and southern hemisphere meet, close to the equator, winds become very light and variable; it is known as 'the doldrums'.

Historically, the doldrums were despised and feared by sailors. With only the wind to power them, ships could get stuck for days, even weeks on end. Fresh water supplies would run short, and some crew members became delirious due to extreme thirst and heat.

Samuel Taylor Coleridge's *Rime of the Ancient Mariner* (1798) describes the doldrums:

Day after day, day after day,
We stuck, nor breath nor motion ...

and the anguish it entailed:

Water, water, every where,
Nor any drop to drink.

Measuring the wind

Anemometers are pieces of scientific equipment used to most accurately measure the speed of the wind. Consisting of several small cups, the anemometer rotates and displays the wind speed to the observer.

Wind-speed measuring technology has advanced in recent years, and now hand-held anemometers are available for a few pounds.

At professional weather stations the traditional 'cup' anemometers are gradually being replaced by sonic anemometers. These measure air disturbance to give a more accurate reading of wind speed.

↑ An anemometer is used to measure wind speed.

The Beaufort Scale

There is also a method of estimating wind speed that has been established for over two centuries. It is reliable, doesn't require expensive equipment, and brings a feeling of satisfaction knowing that we can rely on our senses.

In a story of serendipity, the scale has a fascinating history. It was devised by an Irish hydrographer, Francis Beaufort (later to become Rear-Admiral Sir Francis Beaufort) in 1805. It was first used officially during the voyage of HMS *Beagle* (carrying one Charles Darwin as a passenger), which was commanded by Captain Robert FitzRoy. He would later head up a government department which was a forerunner of our modern UK Meteorological Office.

The scale is easy to use and simply requires the observer to look around at everyday objects for a few seconds. From this one can estimate the wind speed and more reliably make an estimate of the Beaufort force of the wind.

You will hear 'Beaufort forces' used in the shipping forecast, with the higher forces, and hence faster speeds, referred to by name: 'gale force eight'; 'severe gale force nine'; 'storm force ten'; 'severe storm force eleven'; 'hurricane force twelve'.

Have a go at using the scale shown on pages 54–55. Notice the land conditions, check the corresponding wind speed and you should be able to confidently work out what level of wind you're experiencing on the Beaufort scale.

BEAUFORT WIND SCALE

Number	Description	Wind speed	Wave height	Sea conditions
0	Calm	< 1 knot < 1 mph < 2 km/h	0 ft 0 m	Sea like a mirror
1	Light air	1–3 knots 1–3 mph 2–5 km/h	0–1 ft 0–0.3 m	Ripples
2	Light breeze	4–6 knots 4–7 mph 6–11 km/h	1–2 ft 0.3–0.6 m	Small wavelets
3	Gentle breeze	7–10 knots 8–12 mph 12–19 km/h	2–4 ft 0.6–1.2 m	Large wavelets
4	Moderate breeze	11–16 knots 13–18 mph 20–28 km/h	3.5–6 ft 1–2 m	Small waves
5	Fresh breeze	17–21 knots 19–24 mph 29–38 km/h	6–10 ft 2–3 m	Moderate waves
6	Strong breeze	22–27 knots 25–31 mph 39–49 km/h	9–13 ft 3–4 m	Large waves
7	High wind, moderate gale, near gale	28–33 knots 32–38 mph 50–61 km/h	13–19 ft 4–5.5 m	Sea heaps up
8	Gale, fresh gale	34–40 knots 39–46 mph 62–74 km/h	18–25 ft 5.5–7.5 m	Moderately high waves
9	Strong/severe gale	41–47 knots 47–54 mph 75–88 km/h	23–32 ft 7–10 m	High waves
10	Storm, whole gale	48–55 knots 55–63 mph 89–102 km/h	29–41 ft 9–12.5 m	Very high waves
11	Violent storm	56–63 knots 64–72 mph 103–117 km/h	37–52 ft 11.5–16 m	Exceptionally high waves
12	Hurricane force	≥ 64 knots ≥ 73 mph ≥ 118 km/h	≥ 46 ft ≥ 14 m	Exceptionally high waves, sea is completely white

Land conditions
Smoke rises vertically
Direction shown by smoke drift
Wind felt on face
Leaves and small twigs in constant motion
Raises dust and loose paper
Small trees and leaves begin to sway
Large branches in motion
Whole trees in motion
Twigs break off trees
Slight structural damage
Trees uprooted, considerable structural damage
Widespread damage
Devastation

FACTS ABOUT WIND

1 The highest gust of wind recorded at a low-level weather station in the British Isles was on 13 February 1989 when 142mph was registered at Fraserburgh in Aberdeenshire, Scotland.

2 Other planets have winds too; on Saturn winds reach 1,100mph.

3 Some offshore wind farms around the British Isles cover areas of over 115 square miles; that's about 40,000 football pitches.

WEATHER LORE – TRUE OR FALSE?

Unsurprisingly, sailors used to be the most prolific observers of wind, and therefore much wind weather lore flowed from their sayings. Farmers, too, passed on many weather rhymes and proverbs, several of which still have their uses today.

'When March blows its horn, your barn will be filled with grain and corn'

This saying suggests that thunderstorms (the 'horn') in March promise a fine harvest come autumn. While thunderstorms at this time of year would be an indicator of warmer-than-average weather, together with a good supply of water for the growing crops, it says nothing about the weather for the rest of the summer and therefore the success of the harvest.

Can shooting stars predict a change in the direction of the wind?

Sailors used to believe that if you saw a shooting star, the wind would shift to the direction in which the star was travelling. This was one of a number of meanings sailors would attribute to the phenomenon. Some believed a shooting star to the right of a ship was a good omen, while one to the left was a sign of misfortune to come. Interestingly, in recent years Dutch physicist Rosmarie De Wit has been observing the trails from shooting stars that are too small to be seen with the naked eye, and higher in the atmosphere than can be reached by weather balloons, to measure wind data and improve atmospheric weather forecasting.

'A veering wind fair weather, a backing wind foul weather'

Often when the wind changes in a clockwise or 'veering' direction (say from 8 o'clock to 11 o'clock, so westerly to northerly), this can indicate that the weather is going to improve, possibly due to an increase in atmospheric pressure such as a ridge. The opposite is true when the wind direction changes in an anti-clockwise or 'backing' direction (say from 9 o'clock to 6 o'clock), and can indicate that pressure is going to fall and that poorer conditions, and perhaps stronger winds, are on the way.

'The winds of the daytime wrestle and fight, longer and stronger than those of the night'

Winds tend to be stronger during daylight hours, and the daily range of wind speeds increase as temperatures lift during the day, then fall in the evening and overnight as the temperatures fall again. Add to this the gusts which can develop due to daytime heat and there can be notably stronger, gustier winds during the day compared to overnight.

'If birds fly low, expect rain and a blow'

We know that air pressure certainly does affect birds. Swallows, for instance, have sensitive hearing, and when barometric pressure drops they will fly as near to the ground as possible, where air density is at its greatest. Therefore, low-flying birds are generally a sign of imminent rain, while high-flyers indicate fair weather. Moist weather will also encourage insects to swarm and birds that feed on them will fly low to intercept them.

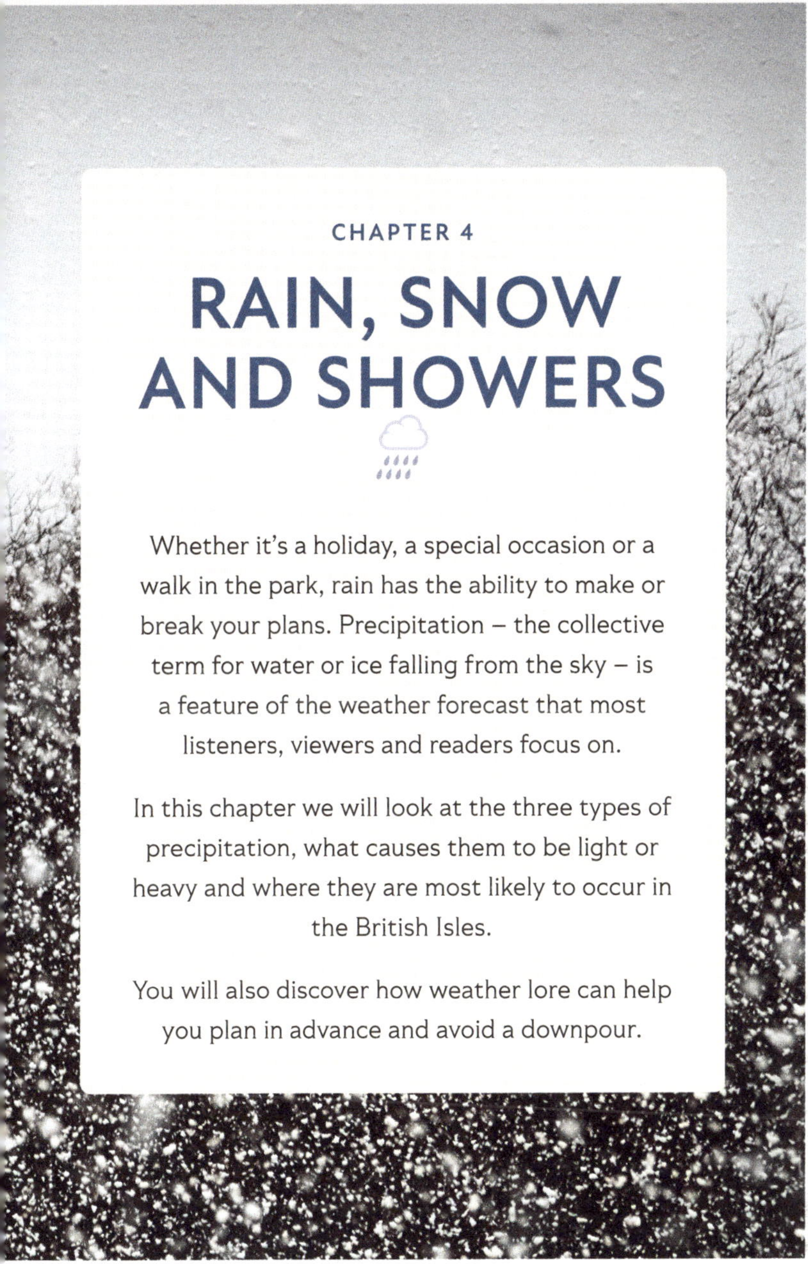

CHAPTER 4

RAIN, SNOW AND SHOWERS

Whether it's a holiday, a special occasion or a walk in the park, rain has the ability to make or break your plans. Precipitation – the collective term for water or ice falling from the sky – is a feature of the weather forecast that most listeners, viewers and readers focus on.

In this chapter we will look at the three types of precipitation, what causes them to be light or heavy and where they are most likely to occur in the British Isles.

You will also discover how weather lore can help you plan in advance and avoid a downpour.

Rain

Clouds form when air is forced to rise. The rising air cools as it goes up through the troposphere; eventually, condensation of water vapour occurs at certain temperatures and we see this as cloud.

The droplets of water within the cloud grow and eventually cannot be sustained by the upward moving air. They fall to the ground because of the effect of gravity, but as they go they crash into other droplets. These are raindrops, which grow larger and eventually fall to earth, striking us, our car windscreens or anything that gets in the way of them.

The heaviness of rainfall depends on how moist the air is, the temperature of the air and the depth of the cloud. In thunderstorms rain will often be heavy, whilst on a weather front the rain may well just be light or moderate.

Rain intensity can be enhanced by the air being forced to rise upwards over hills or mountains. We know this as 'orographic rainfall'. A benign-looking weather front, producing only light rain, can often intensify as the air associated with it rises over hills. In the British Isles we see this effect readily over areas such as western Wales, the western Pennines in England, western areas of the Highlands, Grampians and Southern Uplands in Scotland, as well as on high ground in Northern Ireland and the Republic of Ireland.

Snow

A beautiful, fresh white covering of snow is the stuff of childhood dreams, but, as we are all too aware, the snow rapidly gets dirty once fallen and it isn't long before we are wishing for it to be gone.

In the British Isles snow is a feature of winter weather. It's much less frequent than it once was, although all areas still tend to get at least a day of lying snow during the winter. As one heads further north the number of snow days increases significantly.

The height of terrain also plays a major part in determining how much snow an area sees. Travel anywhere in the British Isles on a winter's day and, given relatively average temperatures for the time of year, snow will be on the tops of the mountains of Wales, northern England, Scotland and Ireland.

Snowflakes begin their life as tiny crystals that form within clouds. The more moist the air, the better those crystals are at sticking

together. They 'grab' each other like magnets, eventually growing large enough to develop into what we see as a snowflake.

The perfect temperature for the formation of a snowflake is around 0°C as this causes the edges of the flake to melt, encouraging other flakes to stick to it and grow ever bigger. Large snowflakes, floating slowly to earth, looking like upside-down parachutes are a good example of this process occurring.

Generally snow will fall when the air temperature is below 2°C or 3°C (the air above the ground doesn't need to be below 0°C for a snowflake to stay frozen). If the temperature is warmer, then a raindrop will fall to the ground instead – although this may freeze as it hits a frozen surface and is then called 'freezing rain'.

If the air is very cold, say below 5°C, then flakes tend to be smaller and don't stick together very well. This snow is easily blown around by the wind in a whirling dust-like state. In air that's closer to 0°C the flakes are bigger and are more likely to gather in drifts, again blown by the wind. This wetter type of snow sticks together well and is perfect for making snowballs and snowmen; drier snow generally falls apart.

Being positioned at the eastern extreme of the North Atlantic does have its benefits for the weather in our islands. The warm ocean, aided by the eastern extension of the North Atlantic Current (North Atlantic Drift), helps to warm our climate, ensuring that things only get really cold in exceptional circumstances.

It's interesting to compare the climate in the British Isles to that of Canada, where Toronto is significantly further south than the British Isles but has much colder, snowier winters.

Much snow in the British Isles falls ahead of warm fronts, leading to a few hours of snow before turning to rain as milder weather arrives. Snow showers (see below) tend to bring short-lived bursts of snow, although these can be heavy and most frequently occur over northern and eastern coasts and hills in northerly airstreams.

Showers

We colloquially think of showers as short-lived periods of rain and snow, perhaps interspersed with drier weather and sunny spells. When forecasters on radio or television mention 'showers', this is exactly what they mean. However, for certain sectors, such as aviation, the term 'shower' has a specific meaning. It refers to precipitation that's falling from a convective cloud, such as cumulus or cumulonimbus.

Showers develop in the same way as thunderstorms (as we will see in the next chapter), although the process of formation doesn't reach such a dramatic conclusion.

FACTS ABOUT RAIN AND SNOW

1 It's never 'too cold to snow', but as cold air holds less moisture snow tends to be lighter.

2 The UK sees an average of 13 days of lying snow each year.

3 Rain occurs on around 164 days each year in the British Isles.

Rising air, relatively warm compared to its surroundings, cools as it rises and therefore condenses. As we have seen before, the condensing process forms water vapour that turns to liquid droplets that then become clouds. If the air surrounding the warm air is cooler then the air will continue to rise, enhancing the cumulus cloud. Eventually the droplets become too large and overcome the upward motion of the air, falling to the ground as rain. It can be that showers are heavy and eventually the cumulus grows into cumulonimbus cloud, perhaps causing hail or thunder.

For most purposes it's fine to think of a shower as a short-lived period of rain, lasting between 10 minutes and an hour.

Forecasting a shower in a specific location is very difficult. It's much easier to suggest a broader area where showers could occur. According to the Met Office, the average shower will only cover $64km^2$ (or 0.026% of the UK) in the time it lasts. The challenge for forecasters, therefore, is to identify that area accurately.

These Met Office statistics demonstrate the difficulty of forecasting showers for a single location and explain why weather apps struggle to do this (see Chapter 9).

4 The average size of a raindrop is approximately 1mm (less than one twenty-fifth of an inch).

5 The wettest day in the UK, with records which date back to 1891, was 3 October 2020, when 7.4 cubic kilometres of water fell, which the UK Met Office says was more than the capacity of Loch Ness.

WEATHER LORE – TRUE OR FALSE?

We've seen that there's a scientific difference between rain and showers; the latter falls from fluffy convective clouds while the former is often associated with fronts. But even before this distinction was established, people were able to make surprisingly accurate predictions of local weather by watching how clouds developed.

'Rain before seven, fine before eleven'

Although this is a popular saying, in scientific terms it is more a statement about how long a typical period of rain from a frontal system may last, which is usually about four hours. So, this can apply at any time of day, not just between seven and eleven. However, depending on other conditions, such as a lack of wind, a front may remain for longer than four hours.

'Red sky at night, shepherd's delight; red sky in the morning, shepherd's warning'

Invoked by Jesus Christ in the gospel of St Matthew (although citing sailors rather than shepherds), this popular rhyme does have a basis in science. A red sunset indicates that high pressure is coming in from the west, which promises fine weather to come. However, a red sky in the morning means that the high-pressure system has passed through and a low-pressure system, possibly with wet and windy weather, is moving in.

The insect weather forecast

Nature can reveal the onset of wetter weather ahead. Ants become more active as atmospheric pressure decreases, perhaps because they detect the lower pressure and hence an increased risk of rain in the coming hours. A drop in pressure may also make bees more active, or even more aggressive, before they return to and remain in the hive. Once rain has passed and pressure rises again, the bees return to foraging.

If the daisies in your garden are closed, don't hang out your washing – it's going to rain

Flowers are sensitive to light levels and many of us will have observed petals closing as the sun sets or disappears behind clouds. Plants are also sensitive to pressure changes and so a flower whose petals close as clouds increase is also 'anticipating' rain ahead. The scarlet pimpernel (*Anagallis arvensis*) is known as 'poor man's weather-glass' as its flowers close tightly when atmospheric pressure falls and open again only when sunny weather is imminent.

Can it be too cold to snow?

The colder the air gets, the less water vapour it contains, reducing the likelihood of snow. Of course, things are never that simple, and there are many other factors that influence whether or not snow falls, such as wind direction, altitude and surface temperatures.

CHAPTER 5

THUNDERSTORMS, LIGHTNING AND HAIL

Severe weather can be awe-inspiring and frightening – foreboding, dark cloud followed by a dramatic flash of lightning.

Lightning can strike throughout the year but is particularly active in summer. Thunderstorms are observed at most weather stations in the UK between 5 and 20 times each year.

A thunderstorm will grow in stages and its life cycle can be clearly witnessed by the attentive skywatcher.

The life of a thunderstorm

As long as conditions are suitable, thunderstorms grow in a well-structured cycle. We'll take a closer look at each stage here.

Stage 1: Growing up

As the sun's rays touch the surface of the Earth, the air heats up. Because the heating is uneven (for example the black tarmac of a car park will become hot more quickly than an adjacent lake), bubbles of warm air form. These are less dense (think 'lighter') than the surrounding air and so begin to rise.

As long as the air that surrounds each bubble remains cooler (see Chapter 2), the bubble will continue to rise. Though still warmer than its surroundings, the bubble of air will cool as it rises.

As the air can only hold a certain amount of water as an invisible vapour for any given temperature, it will eventually have to condense, forming water droplets that we see as clouds.

The warmer a bubble of air is, the more energy it has, and under the right conditions the rising warm air can be strong enough to raise the water droplets even higher into the atmosphere. At the same time, this causes the condensing of any remaining water vapour to form large cumulonimbus clouds (see page 33).

Eventually the water droplets become too large to be held up by the warmer air and they fall to Earth. Due to the amount of water these large cumulonimbus clouds can hold, the rainfall they produce is heavy. However, not all the water droplets fall from the cloud, as we shall see in a moment.

During the growing stage of the cumulonimbus cloud, only **updraughts** (the upward motion) occur. These can be anywhere from 20 to 100 feet per second, so very, very fast!

Stage 2: Here comes the hail

The water droplets that are lifted through the cloud eventually pass through a temperature below freezing and then turn into ice crystals. As more moisture gathers on the droplet or ice crystal it becomes heavier.

As a result of now being heavier, the slushy ice crystal can overcome the upward motion of the warm air and falls through the cloud. The ice crystal meets ever-warmer air as it descends, causing it to thaw. The warmer air will strengthen the updraughts and the droplet rises again, cooling as it goes.

Once more the droplet freezes. A little bit like an onion skin, the droplet has another layer of frozen liquid (or near liquid) water wrapped around it. This is now a hailstone.

The hailstone may go up and down in the cloud many times, thawing and refreezing, and as it does so it hits other hailstones and water droplets. The colliding hailstones generate a negative charge, having rubbed against smaller positively charged ice crystals.

An area of negative charge forms at the bottom of the cumulonimbus cloud; it's here where hail eventually starts to gather, as the larger hailstones can no longer be lifted high into the cloud. The lighter hailstones can still be taken to upper levels of the cloud and here they create an area of positive charge.

The cloud is now similar to a large battery and wants to discharge. The negative charge at the bottom of the cloud is attracted to the surface of the Earth and eventually, when the charge on the cloud is big enough, it will discharge. We see this as a flash of lightning. The sky rapidly brightens and there may be multiple lightning flashes.

As light moves quicker than sound, we see the lightning first and then hear the thunder. The rapid heating of the air as the lightning strike passes through causes the atmosphere at that point to expand rapidly, almost 'exploding', which we hear as thunder.

Stage 3: It's all over

At some point the updraught in the cloud cannot be maintained. Because of this the cloud cannot continue to grow and so the risk of thunder decreases.

The air falling through the cloud then overtakes the upward motion and the cloud collapses. It could be that rain continues to fall from the cloud for a while, but sometimes all we can see are the near-skeletal remains of a once-giant cumulonimbus.

Types of lightning

There are many variants of lightning, some more dangerous than others, and they reveal much about the inner workings of the cloud they originated from.

Cloud-to-ground lightning

This form of lightning (sometimes known as *forked lightning*) occurs when the cloud discharges into the ground. The dramatic form it takes is what most people think of when they imagine lightning, but it is actually the rarest type.

Looking at very slow-motion film of lightning flashes, it's possible to see that the bottom of the cumulonimbus cloud 'extrudes' what is called a **'leader' stroke**. The leader stroke is then met by a **'streamer' stroke**, which comes up from the ground to meet the leader. Once the connection is made the lightning strike occurs.

This is a dangerous form of lightning; it's the one that can cause damage to property and, in the most extreme instances, endanger life. You might hear this type of lightning referred to as a 'thunderbolt'.

The Met Office website contains guidance on what to do if you find yourself in an exposed location during a thunderstorm. Squatting close to the ground, with hands on knees and head tucked between them, reduces your chances of becoming a target.

Intra-cloud and cloud-to-cloud lightning

In thunderstorms that occur at night we often see 'cloud dancing' between the clouds. As the lightning strike occurs it lights the sky, showing shades of luminous purple, blue and grey. This is sometimes referred to as 'sheet lightning'.

If the discharge takes place between the clouds, or sometimes even within the same cloud, it's known as intra-cloud lightning. If the lightning jumps from one cloud to another then this is cloud-to-cloud lightning.

Ball Lightning

Long seen as a myth, ball lightning is a very rare form of lightning that's described as a floating sphere.

Eye-witness reports of ball lightning describe a sphere with a diameter ranging from a few inches to 3 feet; most reports say the sphere is 4–8 inches. Its duration lasts from a few seconds to several minutes. Many reports occur after a lightning flash (which suggests that many of them are perhaps a memory of the flash in the brain), but others say the lightning appeared simultaneously.

There have been occasions where more than one sphere has been seen. After drifting, usually at walking pace, the ball of lightning has been reported as bouncing off a floor, passing through a wall or window, or simply vanishing.

Reports of ball lightning are controversial and many questions still remain about its existence. But if you see it, take a picture!

Forecasting thunderstorms

Predicting when thunderstorms will happen is easier than forecasting exactly where they will be. It tends to be that general areas, rather than precise locations, are subject to thunderstorms.

Professional forecasters use a suite of tools to help predict where a storm may occur: temperature and moisture forecasts at various heights in the atmosphere, wind direction and speed-change predictions, and many other parameters that are fed into models. These produce a probability forecast of a thunderstorm occurring in a particular area.

However, we don't necessarily need complicated technology to forecast thunderstorms; the human body can sense when a day is thundery.

FACTS ABOUT THUNDERSTORMS

1 Lightning hits the surface of the Earth 44 times every second.

2 Cumulonimbus clouds usually take less than an hour to fully develop.

3 Thunder travels at the speed of sound, about 770mph.

Signs to look for

The atmosphere often 'tells' us it's in a thundery mood. Most thunderstorms occur from spring through to early autumn, the heating of the land triggering the storms.

→ If the morning is starting warm, and the sky is clear, look for the middle-level altocumulus castellanus cloud (see page 30) developing.

These small lumps of cloud start to form turrets as heat increases.

You should also feel the air to be quite humid; the more moist it is, the higher the risk of thunderstorms developing.

← Next, perhaps by mid- to late morning, there will be some fluffy cumulus clouds developing.

↑ The cumulus will grow quickly by midday and this signals that the risk of showers, hail and thunderstorms is increasing.

↓ By early to mid-afternoon the transition to cumulonimbus cloud begins. An anvil-shaped top may appear, but not always. These clouds foretell that thunder and hail may occur. So get ready, the weather is about to put on a show!

WEATHER LORE – TRUE OR FALSE?

In the days before scientific understanding, the sights and sounds of a violent storm must have been terrifying for country and city folk alike. Thor, the ancient Norse god of thunder, was believed to wield his hammer, causing the sky to explode; no one knew when this was going to happen. Therefore, as knowledge was passed between the generations, a wealth of thunderstorm weather lore grew.

'Thunder in spring, cold will bring'

Heavy showers in the British Isles, especially early in the spring, are usually associated with cold winds from the north-west. This cold air brings about the right conditions for large cumulus clouds to grow, eventually turning to cumulonimbus and causing thunderstorms.

'A thunderstorm in April is the end of the hoar frost'

It is better to understand this proverb in terms of how localised a thunderstorm is. Isolated storms, which develop because of warm weather (unlike those formed in the cold north-west airmass mentioned above), suggest that warmer air has already arrived and so the likelihood of frost, already diminishing as shorter nights and warmer days occur, reduces even further.

The Thunder Moon

Although the planets and stars have no impact on our day-to-day weather, our Moon has long been observed as a weather messenger. The full moon in July is known as the Thunder Moon, its name a reference to the warm, stormy days associated with that time of year.

'Sharper the blast, sooner 'tis past'

This phrase is attributed to clergyman Charles Wesley, the prolific 18th-century hymn writer. The jet stream can drive storm systems through an area quickly, with a frontal system able to clear an area within three or so hours, and so it seems that, as the rain arrives, the thunder storm ends. If the jet stream is weaker, or is not over the country at the time of the storm, progress may be slower and the storm will last longer.

'Lightning never strikes twice in the same place'

The idea that something as seemingly random as a lightning strike is unlikely to occur in the same place twice has long been used as a way to comfort those who have been affected by an unusual, sad or tragic event. However, lightning can and will hit the same place more than once. Lightning is a massive discharge of electricity that travels from a cloud to the ground. It will find the most direct route to the ground, favouring tall, conductive or prominent structures, such as trees, the masts of ships or skyscrapers. Once a structure proves to be a good conductor, lightning may strike it multiple times. St Paul's Cathedral in London, for example, has a history of lightning strikes, including one in 1561 that set its spire on fire.

Can you work out how far you are from a thunderstorm?

We see lightning immediately, but the sound of thunder takes about 5 seconds to travel a mile. You can work out how far you are from lightning by using the following guide: 0 seconds between lightning and thunderclap – it's very close, so hopefully you're somewhere safe; 5 seconds behind the lightning is a mile away, 10 seconds is 2 miles away, 15 seconds is 3 miles away, and so on.

CHAPTER 6

MIST AND FOG

As the sun slowly rises on an autumn morning, the ethereal drifting of mist on a newly ploughed field is a sight that stays with you.

It reveals the nature of the lower levels of the atmosphere, close to the surface of the Earth – something that's often invisible, as the transparency of the air we walk through each day is usually dominant.

But when the air cools, or when moisture levels rise, we can finally see the most important constituent of the atmosphere: water vapour.

What causes mist and fog?

As you will read throughout this book, water vapour is a gas; it floats all around us in the air and the amount varies day to day and from place to place. On a hot, humid summer's day we can feel it but we can't see it. We sweat, but it brings no relief as the water evaporating from our bodies struggles to cool us down. Even in the most arid of deserts, water vapour is still present in the air.

For any given temperature the atmosphere can only hold so much water vapour as an invisible gas. If the temperature lowers enough, water vapour will condense and become visible as minuscule water droplets that are lighter than air. They dance around, drifting in any breeze and moving with the micro-currents present in the air. If there are enough of these droplets they start to obscure our view; we see this as mist and, should there be enough water droplets, fog.

But mist and fog are very delicate weather phenomena; even the most minor of changes in temperature, wind speed, humidity and pressure can cause the water to disappear into a vapour or reappear as a visible liquid droplet. Like a perfect recipe, it's the precise combination of these factors that determines whether mist, fog, or neither, develop or disappear.

Temperature is the most critical factor for the formation of mist and fog. The warmer the atmosphere, the more water it can hold as an invisible vapour.

But if the temperature falls, and the ratio of temperature to water vapour hits a critical point (called the 'dew point'), the water vapour changes (condenses) into visible water droplets.

The opposite is true if the temperature rises; the air can now hold more water as a vapour and so if mist or fog has occurred the water droplets disappear, visibility increases and we no longer see mist or fog.

Wind is also an important part of the 'mist/fog' recipe. If the wind speed is above 7mph then the mist or fog will lift into low cloud. If it's below 3mph, all we will see (at least initially) is mist or fog very low to the ground, a phenomenon we call 'shallow fog'.

Calm winds are often associated with mist and fog, but actually the perfect wind speed for the formation of mist and fog is about 3–7mph, causing the gentle movement of leaves and branches.

This wind speed is enough to mix up the air: warm and cold, moist and dry pockets, drifting up and down just above the land surface,

each changing as they do so and assisting the future development, or otherwise, of mist and fog.

Forecasters spend a lot of their time forecasting wind speeds, especially at airports and at sea when these changes in wind speed, sometimes of as little as 1mph, can make the difference between a day being hot and sunny or cold and foggy.

The humidity of the air is also an important ingredient. The more moisture there is in the atmosphere, the higher the risk of mist or fog occurring. Remember that temperature is critical to this, and so the more moisture there is, the higher the temperature needs to be before mist or fog forms.

Humidity may increase because of a change in wind direction, perhaps bringing the air off the sea rather than the land. It could also be because a more moist air mass has drifted into the area (often an air mass that has formed over an ocean), or it could even be as subtle as air drifting over a lake or dew pond, adding just enough water vapour to allow condensation to occur.

Again, the reverse is true if the air becomes drier; this can lead to the mist or fog disappearing. Air becomes drier because it has come from a drier area, just as the wind changes direction to flow off a land mass.

So you see how many critical factors go into the recipe for mist and fog development, explaining why it's so difficult to forecast and why you will probably hear forecasters refer to 'a risk of mist and fog'. Cooler valleys, warmer slopes, moist sea coves: all are factors in the mist/fog story.

← Shallow fog.

DIY forecasting mist and fog

Forecasting mist and fog is difficult, even for a professional meteorologist. However, 'feeling' the weather and taking notice of the changes around you can give a good idea as to whether mist and/or fog will be forming.

There are different sorts of fog. The most frequent are radiation fog (on a cool morning or evening), advection fog (around coasts) and hill fog (shrouding the tops of hills and mountains). Each forms slightly differently, but each one can be predicted by anyone with a keen eye on the weather.

Radiation fog

For this fog we typically need temperatures to decrease. It usually occurs during the coolest parts of the day – in the morning, in the evening and overnight.

Look for clear skies during these times. When the sun has set, heat can rapidly radiate away from the ground (hence the name 'radiation fog') and the temperature will fall.

If the wind is light enough (the sweet spot being between 3–7mph)

there will be just enough mixing of the air to mean that it cools in the bottom few feet of the atmosphere, close to the ground.

The amount of water vapour in the air is then important. This varies, but is very much dependent upon where the air has come from. If the winds have been light in the day and the air has been over the land, there probably won't be as much moisture and so the chance of fog forming is reduced; if anything does form, it's likely to be mist.

If the air is more moist, perhaps coming from over the sea or close to a source of water such as a lake, river or stream, this may add enough moisture to meet the critical threshold for mist and fog formation. Usually the greatest likelihood of fog is within an hour or two of sunset and up to an hour or two after sunrise.

On a weather chart (see Chapter 8) look for high pressure as these are often areas where light winds and clear skies occur.

The fog will clear when the temperature rises, the wind speed increases or the air becomes drier – basically the recipe in reverse!

Advection or sea fog

Don't panic! It sounds technical but all 'advection fog' refers to is a warmer (or colder) block of air passing over a colder (or warmer) area of water. This type of fog usually manifests itself as fog over the coasts or sea.

Advection fog can occur inland as well, usually during the winter months as warm air, often from the Atlantic, drifts across the British Isles. This will be familiar as those murky, foggy, drizzly days when it barely gets light and we long for the arrival of spring and summer. The most affected areas are the western coasts of England, Wales and Scotland, but when the wind is in the east, the coasts of eastern Scotland and England are also susceptible.

It's hard for us to look for the signs of advection fog, except on weather charts (see Chapter 8). Advection fog tends to occur behind warm fronts (the red semicircles on weather charts – see page 105) and ahead of cold fronts (the blue triangles) in the area we call the 'warm sector'. If you're within a warm sector, then you know there's a high risk of coastal and sea fog occurring, as well as more extensive fog inland if it's winter.

FACTS ABOUT FOG

1. Temperature, wind and humidity are critical when forecasting mist and fog.
2. Cooler temperatures lead to condensation and the chance of fog increasing.
3. If the wind speed is too high or too low, fog won't occur; 3 to 7mph is perfect.

Hill fog

Hill fog happens when moist air gets forced to rise up and over higher ground. As the air is forced upwards it cools (remember the atmosphere usually cools as we climb) and so this drop in temperature means that water can no longer be held as a vapour. It condenses into water droplets and this is what we see as hill fog: simply cloud that shrouds the tops of hills.

For hill fog to form, first of all the air needs to be moist. If the slope is facing the wind, the air is forced up and over the hill or mountain, and as it reaches its dew point we will see the fog. So see which way the wind is blowing: if it's against the slope, and it's moist, there's a higher chance of fog developing over the hill or mountain.

Often air flowing off the sea, or over another source of water, is moist and more likely to be 'fogable'.

Take extra care if you plan to walk in the hills or mountains when the air is moist, as hill fog can form quickly. All that's needed is for moisture to change slightly and fog can form in minutes, disorientating the unwary walker and leading to a fall in temperature.

4 If a block of warm or cold air is flowing over cold or warm land, advection fog could form.

5 Moist air and a wind blowing onto a hill or mountain slope can lead to the formation of hill fog, and it can form in minutes.

WEATHER LORE – TRUE OR FALSE?

The world can seem so quiet when mist and fog set in. Water vapour has a curious ability to dampen sound. While we see less of fog than other weather phenomena, much of the lore about it relates to the weather of winter predicting the coming seasons.

'So many mists in March, so many frosts in May'

Under high pressure, conditions can be perfect for mist and fog to form: light winds, clear skies and falling temperatures. If high pressure has built up during late winter, and lasts for several days, this can sometimes indicate that the weather pattern of high pressure is likely to recur. Therefore, if there are mists during March that have developed because of high pressure, after a break in weather during April the high pressure may return in May. However, instead of mist forming overnight, temperatures may be low enough to give frosts, which can be a real problem for farmers and gardeners alike.

'When mists take to the hill, then good weather it doth spill. When the mist takes to the sea, then good weather it will be'

This Scottish proverb refers to mist (cloud) shrouding hills, and that when it does so, it's a sign of rain in the hours ahead (the 'spill'). By contrast, when the mist is over the sea this is often associated with milder weather, especially in the summer months. Warm air flowing over the sea can develop sea fog, which drifts onto coasts before breaking up and giving fine, warm days.

‘If there be damp fog or mist, accompanied by wind, expect rain’

A spell of mist or fog during the winter months will often clear as winds increase. Usually this is ahead of fronts that will bring rain, pushing away the mist or fog and leading to more unsettled weather.

‘Grey mists at dawn, the day will be warm’

If we wake up to a misty morning during the summer, we might assume that the day ahead is likely to be a damp one. However, even if there is mist around, if the sky above is blue then you’re observing what is known as a radiation mist, where a layer of cool air is hovering above the ground. It won’t be too long before the heat of the sun warms both the land and the air, and the mist evaporates.

‘A winter fog will freeze a dog’

This saying refers to the bitter cold weather that often accompanies winter fogs. It can also apply to the dense cold air that sits close to the ground in foggy weather, which can quite literally lead to frostbite in a dog’s paws and pain in its legs.

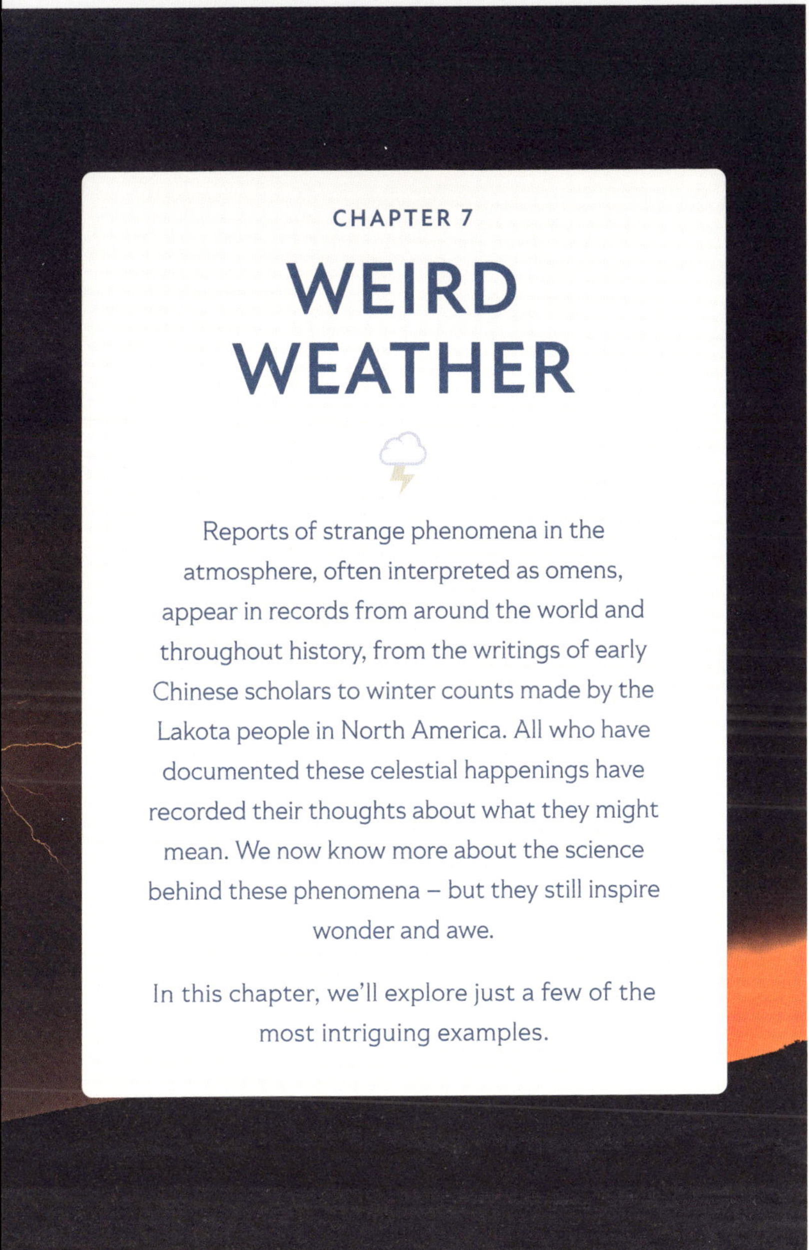

CHAPTER 7

WEIRD WEATHER

Reports of strange phenomena in the atmosphere, often interpreted as omens, appear in records from around the world and throughout history, from the writings of early Chinese scholars to winter counts made by the Lakota people in North America. All who have documented these celestial happenings have recorded their thoughts about what they might mean. We now know more about the science behind these phenomena – but they still inspire wonder and awe.

In this chapter, we'll explore just a few of the most intriguing examples.

Waterspouts

A waterspout is a tornado that occurs over the sea. Waterspouts and tornadoes are formed by the same mechanism of air rising due to convection and subtle changes of wind direction and speed. The vortex of the waterspout or tornado looks very dramatic as it hangs below the cloud.

Close to the sea surface, the bottom of the waterspout shows as a spinning wall of water, which happens as the sea water is blown around by the vortex. The tube itself is made visible by the water being sucked into it.

One of the first signs of a waterspout developing is a dark dot on the surface of the water. A small funnel cloud will initially develop at the cloud base and then extend downwards to the surface of the water, intensifying and spinning further, and eventually forming the waterspout.

These features are an obvious danger to shipping and can be strong enough to tip sailing yachts over and sink them.

Tornadoes

When we think of tornadoes we may imagine scenes of Kansas City from *The Wizard of Oz*. However, they also occur in the British Isles – and more often than you'd think.

The Tornado and Storm Research Organisation (TORRO) is a group that gathers and analyses reports of tornadoes in the UK. The most intense tornado recorded was that of 23 October 1666 in Lincolnshire. It levelled houses to the ground, killed a boy and smashed a church steeple to pieces.

Even to witness the aftermath of a tornado is shocking. I was the first meteorologist on the scene at the Birmingham tornado of 28 July 2005. A wind in excess of 130mph caused serious damage to cars, buildings and trees. I will never forget seeing roofing tiles embedded in trees and vehicles, roofs ripped off and people wandering around in a daze. It was the strongest tornado to hit the country since 1954.

Tornadoes occur when deeply unstable air (warm at the surface and cold higher up) affects the British Isles. It creates deep cumulonimbus clouds and if the winds through the atmosphere change direction and speed just enough, a tornado can form. Often a thunderstorm will be happening at the same time, the tornado shrouded within it.

But despite the stories above, rest assured that most tornadoes in Britain pass without notice; they remain small features hanging below the cloud base and bring little more than gusty winds.

Thundersnow

Although rare, it's possible for thunderstorms to occur in cold weather. Usually such storms happen when a cold air mass arrives from the North Pole or Arctic Ocean. The contrast in temperature between the warmer ocean and the bitterly cold air at high levels allows for large cumulonimbus clouds to develop and thunderstorms to materialise. In such cold, snow can fall from the cumulonimbus cloud instead of rain. This is thundersnow.

Sprites

Pilots have reported the appearance of short-lived red perturbances 'flashing' above a cumulonimbus cloud. Sometimes these 'sprites' can be seen from the ground and phone cameras are perfect for capturing them using long-exposure images.

Sprites appear to be caused by positively charged cloud-to-ground lightning strikes. Research is underway to understand the exact process that causes them.

Sundogs

There are many different types of halos that can form around the sun or moon. The sundog, sometimes called a 'mock sun', is one of the most beautiful. This dazzling display has impressed onlookers throughout history and appears in the writings of Aristotle, Cicero and Seneca.

Caused by the refraction of sunlight by ice crystals, sundogs appear on either side of the sun and are usually accompanied by a halo around the sun too.

The best time to see these is when the sun is low in the sky, but they're visible at any time of the year. You will notice them more when a front is approaching and cirrus or cirrostratus clouds are visible.

Morning Glory

A line of squally (gusty) winds accompanies the Morning Glory cloud, which, although able to form in several regions of the world, appears most frequently and spectacularly in north-east Australia.

Caused by a sea breeze, this is a type of 'roll cloud' that moves rapidly, often at speeds approaching 40mph. As the roll of cloud arrives, winds become squally. There can be a succession of clouds, each bringing a spell of squally winds, but with calmer winds and sunshine between them.

Making for beautiful pictures, the phenomenon, as its name suggests, tends to occur in the mornings and at the end of the dry season, which in north-east Australia is from early September to mid-November.

Glider pilots enjoy chasing this cloud and 'surfing' along it for many miles.

CHAPTER 8

WEATHER MAPS

Weather maps unlock secrets, but to the uninitiated they can look like a cryptic collection of shapes and colours, joined by lines and letters that just add to the mystery.

But with a few pointers and a little insight into what these shapes and colours mean, you can reveal the inner workings of the weather and add to your forecasting knowledge.

From rain to showers and from gales to calm winds, the weather map reveals all.

↑ Meteorological charts and maps for forecasting weather conditions.

There's an assumption from weather presenters, and companies publishing weather maps online, that viewers understand what all these symbols mean. Of course, there's no way every weather bulletin or web page could possibly begin with a full explanation.

The sort of weather map you see will depend where you are looking, but also on what you need to use the information for and what's easiest for you.

It can be confusing, so here's what you need to know.

The pressure is on

Below is how a weather map may look. It can appear complicated as there are many lines marked on it.

First, it's important to know that these charts show pressure and weather fronts.

Areas of high and low pressure are marked on the chart: 'H' denotes a centre of high pressure and 'L' denotes a centre of low pressure. These are the highest and lowest pressures relative to the air that's around them.

There's no pressure number at which high pressure becomes 'high' or low pressure becomes 'low'; both are relative to the pressure of the air that surrounds them. So how do we measure pressure?

↓ A UK Met Office weather map.

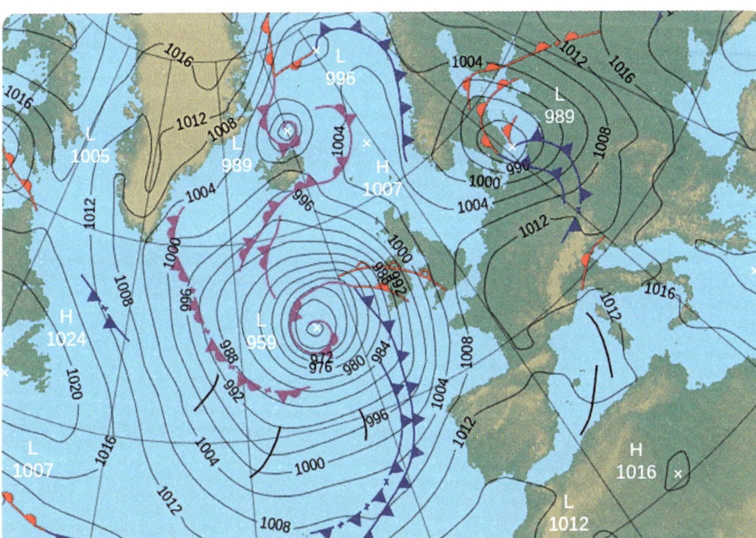

The solid black lines on the chart are **isobars** (the shorter, thicker black lines are known as troughs - see page 116). These lines join points where the same pressure is being reported. (The relevance of isobars is explained later in this chapter.)

Now, imagine you walked up a hill and took a barometer with you. Pressure would fall as you climbed up the hill because the density of the air decreases with height. If we tried to compare the pressure from different weather stations at different heights, we would get some very strange-looking isobars. The pressure falls at a rate of about 1 millibar for every 27 feet we climb in the lower levels of the troposphere.

Knowing this we can make a calculation to reduce the pressure read at a weather station to sea level, creating a common baseline. We can then compare pressure readings for weather stations (using the assumption they're all at sea level, which we know they're not).

Then we join these lines of equal pressure to give us the isobars shown on the chart; this is called Mean Sea Level Pressure (MSLP).

Winds and pressure

As well as telling what the pressure is, isobars also give much information about winds.

Winds flow in an anticlockwise direction around areas of low pressure and in a clockwise direction around high pressure. Look at the weather map on page 105. Imagine the winds flowing around the area of low pressure if you are based in the British Isles. We can estimate that the wind is blowing from the south.

The isobars also inform the viewer about the strength of the winds. Measuring the distance between the isobars, a forecaster can get a very accurate estimation of what the wind speed is likely to be at any given point.

But we don't need to make that precise measurement to forecast whether the winds are strong or not. That's because the closer together the isobars are, the stronger the winds are likely to be.

Again looking at the weather map (see page 105), you can see how the isobars are much closer together over Ireland than over the east of England and Scotland. We can therefore say that there were stronger winds in Ireland, and in fact the winds over Ireland were gale force, whereas in the east of England and Scotland the winds were much lighter.

High pressure

In areas of high pressure, marked by the 'H' symbols on the map, the weather is generally seen to be fair. Winds are usually light and skies are clear. By day there may be plenty of sunshine.

High pressure forms because the air is sinking. This may be due to a certain set of winds at high levels, or just because there's nothing to sustain upward motion in the air. Imagine someone is pushing downwards on your shoulders; you would feel pressure, and hence we term this 'high pressure'.

In the summer the sunshine brings hot weather, but during a winter's night that combination of light winds and clear skies can lead to frost and fog. In the British Isles high pressure (also sometimes called an **anticyclone**) that has been hanging around for some time can become 'dirty'. It fills with pollution and, if there's no wind to disperse this, cloud can form. Especially in the winter months, mist and fog get trapped underneath the high pressure area bringing dark, damp, cold days.

Low pressure

Low pressure areas, marked with an 'L' on the weather map (see page 105), are usually associated with unsettled weather. It's in these areas that air is rising, cooling, condensing and forming cloud and rain.

Most of the time low pressure moves west to east across the Atlantic and will be giving spells of rain, often followed by showers.

Winds tend to be strong in areas of low pressure, as the contrasts between warm and cold air are at their greatest. The boundary between these warm and cold areas of air becomes stronger, increasing the wind further and also lowering pressure even more – we say the area of low pressure is 'deepening'.

The deeper an area of low pressure is, generally the worse the weather may be: more cloud, wind and rain.

Weather fronts

Think of these as areas of cloud and rain. Because warm and cold air don't mix well, the boundary between these two air masses becomes sharp. The temperature contrast, which is greatest in low pressure (see above), helps in the formation of cloud and rain, hence why it's in low pressure areas that we see fronts.

Each type of front – warm, cold and occluded – has its own sequence of clouds and weather associated with it.

Warm fronts tend to be about 200 miles from the first wispy high-level cirrus clouds until the front passes. Behind the warm front we find an area called the 'warm sector'.

Following a warm front is usually a cold front. These tend to bring heavier rain and are about 75 miles across.

Warm fronts are slow moving whilst cold fronts move more quickly. The cold front eventually catches up with the warm front, and where the two meet is what we know as the 'occluded front'.

Occluded fronts tend to be about 150 miles across and bring areas of moderate rain.

Warm fronts

Shown on the weather map by solid semicircles (coloured red on the map on page 105), the warm front marks the boundary between cool air ahead and warmer air behind. The semicircles point in the general direction in which the front is heading, so on our map the warm front over Ireland is heading in a north-easterly direction.

The first sign of the warm front approaching will be high-level cirrus cloud. This thickens and lowers, forming medium-level altocumulus and altostratus. It's from this cloud that we get the first rain of the front. The rain may be light at first but, as the front gets close, cloud will be thickening and the rain turns more persistent. It's rare to get heavy rain on a warm front; most rain is moderate. This comes from nimbostratus cloud that occurs just ahead and along the warm front. All the time a warm front approaches, pressure will be falling.

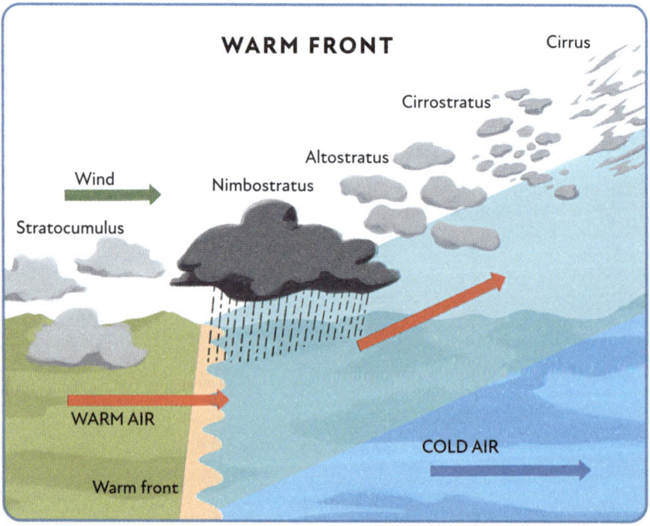

Once it has passed, temperatures rise, the wind changes direction and the rain turns more drizzly. Very often low stratus cloud arrives. This low cloud may shroud hills and coasts facing the wind.

In most frontal systems a cold front follows; the area between the warm front and cold front where the low cloud is occurring is the 'warm sector'.

Cold fronts

Denoted by the triangles (coloured blue on the map on page 105), the cold front marks the boundary between warm air ahead of the front and colder air behind. The triangles point in the direction in which the front is heading.

Remember that the cold front is moving more quickly than the warm front. This fast movement further exaggerates the temperature difference between the warm air of the warm sector and the cold air behind the cold front, intensifying the rainfall along the cold front.

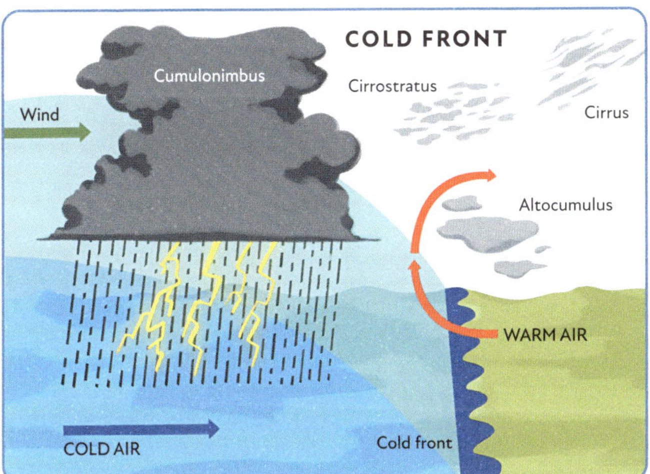

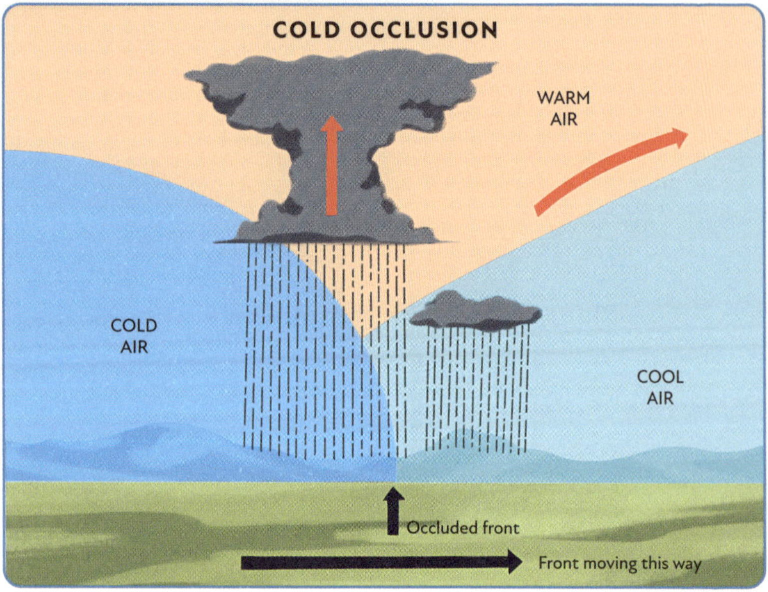
COLD OCCLUSION
WARM AIR
COLD AIR
COOL AIR
Occluded front
Front moving this way

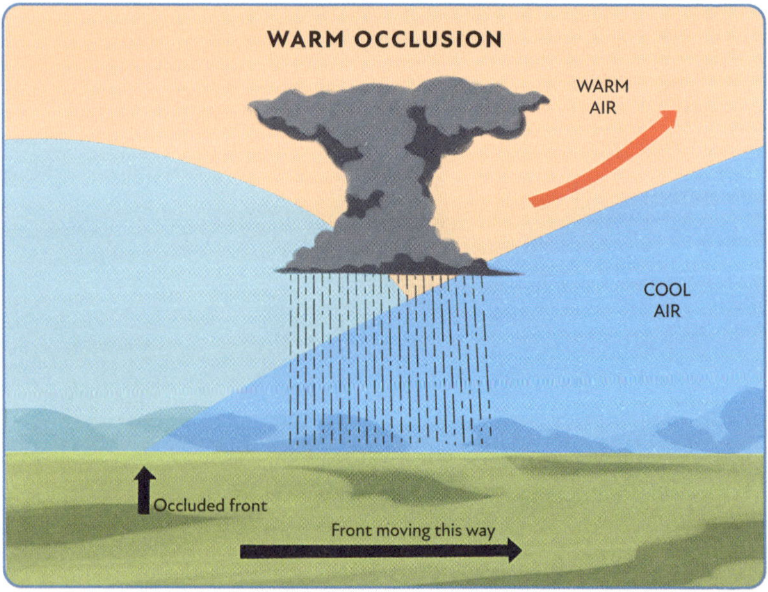
WARM OCCLUSION
WARM AIR
COOL AIR
Occluded front
Front moving this way

Gusts of wind may occur as the front passes through. There could even be a crack of thunder as the warm air is rapidly scooped up by the faster-moving cold air, allowing deep clouds to form. Rain may be heavy, although it will not be lasting too long.

As the cold front passes the temperature will fall, the wind changes direction and pressure will rise.

Behind the cold front is an area known as the 'cold sector'. At first the weather behind the cold front is often fine, with sunshine – a relief after the rain. However, within an hour or two clouds will be seen forming, possibly growing into large cumulus or cumulonimbus, allowing showers to develop, which become ever heavier.

Occluded fronts

Shown by semicircles and triangles together (purple on our map on page 105), occluded fronts tend to be more varied in their weather and cloud patterns. The marks along the front point generally in the direction in which the front is heading.

There's no real sequence of cloud associated with an occlusion; rather the meeting of the cold air with the warm air lifts this warm air above the surface, causing nimbostratus clouds to form and rain to fall. The rain along an occluded front can be heavy at times and tends to straddle the front. As the front passes, conditions may quickly turn showery, some of which may be heavy.

Temperature changes vary, depending on how the occluded front has formed.

Troughs

Solid black lines shown on the weather map (see page 105), without any semicircles or triangles marked on them, are known as troughs.

These are concentrated areas of heavy showers, often associated with large cumulus or cumulonimbus clouds that can group together to give a line of showers, usually around 50 miles across. Because of the depth of the clouds, thunder and hail are possible.

The area both ahead and behind the trough is usually associated with good weather.

Where to find weather maps

Weather maps with fronts marked on them can be hard to find. However, those at Weatherweb.net (the author's own site) and the Met Office are reliable and the charts are regularly updated:

Weatherweb.net
premium.weatherweb.net/models/ukmo-fronts/

Met Office
weather.metoffice.gov.uk/maps-and-charts/surface-pressure

FACTS ABOUT WEATHER MAPS

1 Clouds associated with the fronts drawn on a weather map can have a depth of 15,000 feet on a warm front, and as much as 30,000 feet on a cold front.

2 The classic diagrams of fronts were established by the Bergen School of Meteorology in Norway at the end of the First World War.

3 Hills and mountains can 'destroy' fronts, causing all of the moisture within them to 'rain out'. This gives rise to a 'weak' front.

CHAPTER 9

WEATHER FORECASTS

Until the advent of the internet, one had to make a conscious effort to listen to weather forecasts on the radio, watch them on television or read them in newspapers. Access to forecasts is now much easier. Clicking a weather app on a mobile phone is enough to return an hourly forecast for your exact location two or more weeks ahead.

But how are these forecasts made and which ones can we trust?

Traditional forecasting

The history of forecasting goes back to a time when the only signs we had of the forthcoming weather were in the trees, the sky and, somewhat inaccurately, the stars. Such weather signs evolved into weather lore, some of the sayings proving to be more accurate than others.

In earlier chapters we looked at weather lore that can still be used to forecast conditions for the coming hours and days. These sayings and observations evolved over millennia of humans watching, observing and passing on their wisdom to new generations.

Until the late 1800s, this passed-down knowledge was all we had to help us make forecasts – although the manufacture of scientific instrumentation during the 1600s had enabled increasingly accurate observations of weather conditions, and the first regular rainfall records in the British Isles were logged by the mid-1700s.

In the late nineteenth century, the arrival of the wireless telegraph enabled people to transmit weather observations quickly around the world. It was then possible to draw up charts of weather and, by using scientific techniques, to establish rules for forecasters to follow when making predictions.

← 'Red sky at night, shepherd's delight'.

Along came computers

Empirical methods were in sole use until the arrival of computers in the 1950s. One of the first applications of computers was in weather forecasting. As computers became faster, ever-more complicated calculations could be made and what we now know as 'models' became established.

These models could take in massive amounts of data and rapidly analyse it. By applying equations, including those of motion and thermodynamics, models could make calculations of locations across the globe, assessing each one for the knock-on effect that calculation would have on a neighbouring location.

As computers became more powerful, they could make calculations for more locations and further in advance. Not only that, but the calculations they made would be available more quickly.

The calculations computers make are turned into data, which can be converted to weather charts and then made available to trained meteorologists. Since the internet came along in the 1990s, the information has been made available to all who have access to it.

An international enterprise

The size and expense of the computers needed to produce weather forecasts has risen exponentially. Therefore, only weather services funded by national governments tend to operate computer models.

Each weather model may operate slightly differently, from the weighting given to each equation to the area covered by it.

As weather knows no international boundaries it's vital that countries share weather information freely between each other. The only time this doesn't happen is when countries are at war.

↖ Monitoring Cyclone Dana at the India Meteorological Department in Delhi in October 2024.

↓ Storm Babet lashes Seaham Lighthouse in County Durham in October 2023.

The future of forecasting

As with so many areas of technology, weather forecasting is undergoing rapid change thanks to artificial intelligence (AI) and machine learning (ML).

These require even more powerful computers, but as AI 'learns' more about the model it's using, the theory is that forecasting should get better.

Initial signs are good. Data from the European Centre for Medium-Range Weather Forecasts (ECMWF) has shown that its AI model has performed better than its traditional mathematical model, and no doubt as you read this further advancements are being made.

One of the major steps forward in using AI is that complicated, detailed forecasts can now be made on a regular laptop and in a matter of minutes.

How about human forecasters?

Humans do still have a part to play in the weather forecast.

One of the downsides of the availability of so much information is that those subtle differences between forecasts can sometimes be confusing. Models can make large changes in the forecast each time they're started. A model has a definite answer; it isn't good at subtleties.

Human weather forecasters have a depth of experience gained by observing weather situations over many years. They get to know the strengths and weaknesses of various models and the weather situations in which they perform best.

Computers are also not that good at writing forecasts in a style that is accessible to the general public. When creating a specific forecast, humans can give various scenarios and communicate them in a way that is more understandable.

To borrow an economic phrase, human meteorologists still 'add value' to the weather forecast.

↑ Storm Mathis approaching the UK in March 2023.

← AI forecasting at Shanghai New Expo Center in July 2025.

Which forecasts should you trust?

With forecasts now available from so many sources, it can be tricky to establish which are the best.

There's still no substitute for a forecast prepared and communicated by a human being, though these tend to be rather rare these days. The ones at Weatheronline (weatheronline.co.uk), the author's own site, and the Met Office (metoffice.gov.uk) offer some of the best and most comprehensible forecasts available to the public.

But with so few forecasts by humans, it's often necessary to turn to those available on mobile phone apps or online.

↓ Snow settles over Painswick in Gloucestershire.

↑ Flooding across the Somerset Levels near Langport.

Forecasts on mobile phones or online

Most of these forecasts are automatically produced by computers 'looking' at the output from a model and then translating this into a readable forecast of symbols and numbers. However, the computer is only looking at absolute data. It cannot make any assessment as to the likelihood of an event happening, or be subtle in describing the weather changes that may occur.

Parameters such as wind direction are usually pretty accurate, but when it comes to weather, especially on showery days, the user should be very sceptical. Beyond a guess at the broad geographical area, it's almost impossible for an atmospheric model to predict where a shower will occur.

Claims of making an hourly, accurate forecast for a specific postcode are unfounded and something to be wary of. Such forecasts are best used as a guide. They are fine if an inaccurate forecast is going to do no more than get the washing wet. However, for more important decisions you should be very wary of trusting them.

Presented forecasts

Some forecasts, available from sites such as the BBC (bbc.co.uk/weather) and Met Office (metoffice.gov.uk), still have the benefit of being written and presented by a human forecaster.

Whether online or on television, the presenter can assess data from more than one model and then, even though presenting graphics from a specific model, elaborate on these forecasts to convey uncertainties and possible alternatives.

Time constraints mean that it isn't feasible for every town and village to be given its own forecast, but the skill of the presenter is to provide enough information for the viewer to make an educated assessment as to what may happen.

These are still the best forecasts available as they give plenty of information in an easy-to-understand format. You just need to know where the place you are interested in is located on the map!

↑ Parched grass at the New Forest in Hampshire following an extended heatwave in 2018 – a sight that's becoming increasingly common in British summers.

WEATHER FORECAST FACTS

1 Vice-Admiral FitzRoy founded the UK Meteorological Office in 1854.

2 A Storm Warning Service, which evolved into what is now known as the Shipping Forecast, first began in 1861.

3 Probably the most famous weather forecast ever made was that of 6 June 1944, D-Day. Accurately forecasting a brief improvement in conditions allowed the invasion to go ahead.

4 The weather forecast computer at ECMWF (see page 124) makes 30 million billion calculations per second.

Index

Acknowledgements

A work such as the one you are reading is the result of a lifetime of accumulated knowledge from many sources. The generosity of those who went before in sharing their experience and knowledge of meteorology and climatology, and in sparking the lightning of interest in the brain of an enthusiastic six-year-old cannot be underestimated. Thanks go to all who have proofread this book and made comments and suggestions; including, but not limited to, Kate (my wife) and the wonderful team at HarperCollins (David Salmo and Peter Taylor) who had patience and kept me to deadlines (almost) and have put together a beautiful book.

Tackling Climate Change

The National Trust cares for places of nature, beauty and history, and the range of ways that climate change can impact what we look after is significant. In the short term, the places we care for face flooding, wildfires, drought and coastal erosion. There are long-term threats, too, such as changing weather patterns disturbing important habitats, and increasingly humid conditions making the conservation of collections more challenging. Changes in our climate will influence all of us, how we travel and what we do with our time. The National Trust's holiday cottages, cafés and shops – vital for people's enjoyment as well as for funding conservation – are also affected by temporary closures as a result of flooding, storms and high heat.

In response, the National Trust is taking a positive, forward-looking approach that puts resilience, evidence and innovation at its heart. We're embedding climate considerations into everyday decisions, guided by research, evidence and lessons from the past, and working with nature wherever possible. Alongside adapting to change, we're cutting carbon emissions, capturing more carbon through land, and aiming for net zero by 2030. By working in partnership and sharing its story, the National Trust is not only protecting nature, beauty and history, but also inspiring collective action so that people and nature can thrive together, now and for generations to come.

We don't have all the answers right now, but we're in a good place to learn more about climate change and find ways to meet the challenges head-on. For further information, visit www.nationaltrust.org.uk/our-cause/nature-climate